IMMORTALITY

OF THE

GODS

IMMORTALITY
OF THE
GODS

Legends, Mysteries, and the
Alien Connection to Eternal Life

NICK REDFERN

IMMORTALITY OF THE GODS
EDITED BY ROGER SHEETY
TYPESET BY PERFECTYPE, NASHVILLE, TENN.
Cover illustration by vril8
Printed in the U.S.A.

To order this title, please call toll-free 1-800-CAREER-1 (NJ and Canada: 201-848-0310) to order using VISA or MasterCard, or for further information on books from Career Press.

The Career Press, Inc.
12 Parish Drive
Wayne, NJ 07470
www.careerpress.com

Library of Congress Cataloging-in-Publication Data
CIP Data Available Upon Request.

ACKNOWLEDGMENTS

I would like to offer my very sincere thanks and deep appreciation to everyone at New Page Books and Career Press, particularly Michael Pye, Laurie Kelly-Pye, Jeff Piasky, Lauren Manoy, Roger Sheety, and Adam Schwartz, and to all the staff at Warwick Associates for their fine promotion and publicity campaigns. And a special thank-you goes out to my literary agent and friend, Lisa Hagan, without whom you would not be reading these words.

CONTENTS

INTRODUCTION

Immortality: it is perhaps the one thing, more than any other, that all of us crave. Each and every one of us is on a time limit, and we're all too aware of that fact. Today, in the United States, the average life expectancy is 78.7 years. In the United Kingdom it's 81. Japan's citizens can expect to reach 83. In January 2015, the UK's *Telegraph* newspaper reported the following: "According to estimates published by the Office for National Statistics the average life expectancy for newborn girls in the UK is on course to reach just under 97 years and four months within just over two decades" (Bingham, 2015). In view of all the above, it will very likely not be too long before it becomes entirely normal for humans to reach a century, and maybe even a bit more than that.

As impressive as all of that certainly sounds, what of the possibility of not just living for a century, but even for more than a few millennia? Even more incredible, try and imagine the concept of never dying, as in *ever*. Is such a seemingly incredible thing really possible? It may not only be feasible, it may very well have been achieved in the distant past. We are talking about ancient extraterrestrials having uncovered the secrets behind slowing, and ultimately completely stopping, the process of aging.

Certainly, history is filled with accounts of fantastic beings, legendary gods, and half-human/half-alien entities, such as demigods,
who are reputed to have had extraordinarily long life spans. Today,
stories of such renowned figures are largely dismissed as nothing more
than the stuff of legend, folklore, and mythology. But, what if that's
not actually the case at all? What if the accounts are all too amazingly
real? If so, who were the all-powerful extraterrestrials that tapped into
the secrets of immortality? Did they, thousands of years ago, choose
to share those same secrets with certain, select humans who—as a
result—spectacularly succeeded in beating the Grim Reaper at his own
game? These and many more are the questions posed in *Immortality of
the Gods*. The highlights include:

- The controversial story of the Anunnaki, the legendary
  space-faring entities that first visited the Earth hundreds
  of thousands of years ago and who—using advanced
  genetics-based technology—effectively created the human
  race. Gene-splicing, interspecies reproduction, and cell
  manipulation all ensured the creation of early humans,
  who ultimately became slaves to their extraterrestrial
  masters. Whereas the Anunnaki had life spans of hundreds of thousands years, early humans—known as the
  Adamu—were deliberately engineered to have extremely
  short life spans. Namely, the depressingly short 70 or so
  years. Indeed, the Bible tells us: "The days of our years
  are three score years and ten; and if by reason of strength
  they be four score years, yet is their strength labor and
  sorrow; for it is soon cut off, and we fly away" (Psalm 90,
  2012). On occasion, however, and as will be revealed, the
  Anunnaki bestowed the secrets of extensive longevity
  on certain humans, including some of the most famous
  figures in the Bible. Zecharia Sitchin, who dug very deeply
  into the history of the Anunnaki, came to believe that

the Anunnaki in their original form may have had life spans approximately the length of ours. However, he also concluded that the Anunnaki learned the secrets of how to prevent cell degradation, how to slow down the aging process, and how to almost stop it completely. Perhaps, one day, we will follow in their path.

- The Bible also informs us that Adam fathered a child at the impressive age of 130, a son who he named Seth. On top of that, Adam had no intention of shuffling off this mortal coil now that Seth was on the scene. In fact, he is said to have lived for another 800 years and fathered even more children. Seth was noted for his longevity, too. Following in the footsteps of his father, he became a father to Enosh at the age of 105 and lived to in excess of 800. Seth lived even longer: to the age of 912. Then there's the matter of Methuselah, who lived to the stunning age of 969, almost one millennium, which is both shocking and jaw-dropping in equal measures. All of this provokes an important question, one which is highly relevant to the story this book tells: how is it that so many Old Testament characters lived close to one thousand years? *Immortality of the Gods* reveals the facts surrounding the stories of the likes of Methuselah, Noah, and Seth, and demonstrates their deep connections to the gods. In reality, those gods were highly advanced ETs—the aforementioned Anunnaki—whose science, medicine, and technology ensured that those famous, biblical figures outlived just about everyone else. We are talking about the likes of the Nephilim, described in the Bible as the offspring of the sons of God (actually the Anunnaki) and the daughters of men.

- The *Epic of Gilgamesh*, a renowned saga penned around 4,000 BC. It describes the story and life of Gilgamesh of the title. He was a mighty Sumerian ruler who held sway over Uruk, a city located in ancient Sumer. Gilgamesh was almost certainly part-human and part-Anunnaki. Or, to use the correct term, one of those aforementioned demigods; one who was human, but who also had a genetic connection to the gods from the stars. Like the Anunnaki themselves, Gilgamesh was a towering and imposing figure, possibly even close to an astonishing 16 feet in height—one of the legendary giants as described in the pages of the Bible. As for his life span, it was certainly extensive: we know that Gilgamesh ruled over the people of Uruk for close to 130 years. That he was not pure Anunnaki, however, ensured that Gilgamesh was not destined for literal life-unending. But, this did not prevent him from trying to seek out the secrets of immortality. He went on a quest to find a fabled character, Utnapishtim, who had achieved Gilgamesh's ultimate goal: everlasting life. The secrets allegedly lay in a mysterious plant that had incredible powers of rejuvenation. For Gilgamesh, unfortunately, the secrets eluded him. That he reigned for around 130 years, however, is a good indicator he was of Anunnaki blood.

- The intriguing matter of the biblical Manna from Heaven and the many and varied worldwide equivalents, such as White Powder Gold, Indian Amrita, and magical Chinese potions of a decidedly mysterious nature. They are all designed with one incredible goal in mind, namely, to combat aging—as in forever. John 6:50–51 tells us that Manna was, essentially, perceived as a form of bread sent from a heavenly realm above. So the story went that ingesting Manna was all but guaranteed to give someone not just an extraordinarily long life span, but even immortality too.

- A study of the claims that one of the reasons for the 2003 invasion of Iraq was to uncover the secrets of White Powder Gold, a Manna-like substance of mysterious proportions that ensures the constant rejuvenation of human cells. It's a story that has its origins in the worlds of the Anunnaki and ancient Iraq, but which quickly jumps forward to the modern era. Jim Marrs, one of the most learned figures in the field of White Powder Gold, says of this issue: "The recent discovery of exotic mona-tomic elements, the ages-long quest for both gold and its alchemical secrets, ancient texts that speak of life-giving powder and the proximity of Iraq to the source of knowledge concerning this certainly provides one possible motive for the invasion and looting of Iraq" (Marrs, 2004). Marrs' theories concerning White Powder Gold and a link between this mysterious substance and immortality and the Anunnaki will be presented.

- The saga of a legendary Celtic god. His name was Manannan mac Lir. Rather notably, he lived in a domain known as the Land of Youth. He was immortal, never fell ill, and his mode of transport was a large craft of the high-seas that sounds very much like a modern-day submarine. As to how he achieved such a state of unend-ing youth, it was all down to the significantly titled Cauldron of Regeneration. Interestingly, Manannan mac Lir's wife was a queen of the fairies. Her name was Fand and, like all fairies, she was near-immortal. UFO researcher Jacques Vallee has noted the deep parallels between today's accounts of so-called alien abduction and centuries-old European tales of the so-called "little people" kidnapping unwary souls on dark nights. From immortal fairies to aliens with incredibly long life spans, there may not be much difference. Indeed, they may very well be one and the same, as we'll see.

• In the 1950s, a number of "contactees" had encounters with alien beings that one can argue were immortal. One such story revolves around a man named Frank Stranges, the founder of the National Investigations Committee on Unidentified Flying Objects. At the height of his UFO research in the 1950s and 1960s, Stranges claimed to have met an extremely human-looking extraterrestrial named Valiant Thor. According to Stranges, Thor eerily resembled actor Michael Rennie's character, Klaatu, in the 1951 movie *The Day the Earth Stood Still*. Stranges learned that numerous human-looking aliens had infiltrated the Pentagon, and even the White House, as part of a concerted effort to try and steer the human race away from the threat of atomic destruction. One solitary photograph of Thor exists. What is particularly intriguing, however, is that no less than seven individuals claim to have had experiences with Thor in the 2000s, and all have stated that Thor appeared not to have aged in the 50–60 years that have passed since Stranges' photograph of Thor was taken.

• On a near-identical path, there is the story of William Mills Tompkins. Now in his 90s, Tompkins worked in the secret world of naval intelligence, the Douglas Aircraft Company, and NASA; it was a career that began in the 1950s and spanned decades. Like Stranges, Tompkins states that he met with numerous human-looking aliens—chiefly women—in the 1950s and in top secret, secure facilities and installations. Notably, claims have been made that these very same women have been encountered in the 2000s. Like Valiant Thor, they have not aged in the slightest.

- The intriguing puzzle of the Count of St. Germain. He was a noted figure in the field of alchemy, who came to prominence in the 1700s and who has become the subject of countless debates. It is said that he walked when Jesus lived, even taunting him as he, Jesus, was about to be crucified. Some say that centuries later the count took on the identity of the son of a Transylvanian prince, Francis II Rakoczi. Voltaire described him as a man possessed of vast knowledge and who had achieved a state of immortality. Micah Hanks says of the enigmatic count that he "carried with him an air of mystique the likes of which none during his lifetime had ever matched, or even neared. It was said by some that Saint Germain was an immortal, and that he had somehow uncovered the secrets to eternal youth" (Hanks, 2013). Notably, Guy Ballard, who created the highly controversial I AM Activity cult, claimed to have met the count on the slopes of Mt. Shasta, California, in 1930—a mountain known for its extensive UFO activity, as well as for claims that it was the final haven for the ancient people of Lemuria, perceived by some researchers as none other than extraterrestrials.

- In 1988, a physicist named Robert Scott Lazar spent several months working at the notorious Area 51 at Groom Lake, Nevada. According to Lazar, while at the top-secret base he was shown a number of recovered UFOs built on another world. Not only that, Lazar was also exposed to numerous files and documents concerning a longstanding alien presence on Earth. Two things in particular stood out for Lazar: (a) he learned that housed at Area 51 was an extremely thick, and highly classified, book that told the true story of humankind's origins and the role played by religion in human development; and (b) he was told that the aliens refer to us as containers. Containers of what? Of souls. The aliens allegedly have the ability to extract the human soul from the physical body at the moment of death and to transfer it into a newborn baby, or even into a growing, unborn fetus. In essence, the aliens provide us with immortality by constantly recycling us into new bodies. Interestingly, John Philoponus (born in Alexandria in 490 and a theologian) believed that the soul does not remember its previous lives. Such a belief was also referenced in the classified material at Area 51. Namely, that each and every one of us achieves immortality, yet we fail to recognize it as we reincarnate with (for the most part at least) no memories of our earlier existences.

- Additional accounts of how the aliens do exactly the same in their species. The alien soul lives forever; however, the body of the iconic Grey alien is actually something akin to a biological robot, into which the alien soul can be inserted. Then, when the genetically created body finally begins to degrade after centuries, the alien soul is transported into a brand new shell. Such a process— a deeply strange kind of immortality—continues ad infinitum.

- Whitley Strieber, one of the world's most well-known alien abductees, asked of his extraterrestrial kidnappers what their role was on Earth. He was told that soul recycling was at the forefront of their presence. The late abduction expert Dr. John Mack compiled an entire dossier on abductees who claimed their souls had been extracted from previous lives the moment of death and inserted into unborn human fetuses—again, demonstrating the immortal nature of the soul, and the aliens' deep knowledge of such issues.

- An examination of why we age. In 2013, Michael D. West, PhD, said of this growing area of research: "When perfected, this technology offered the theoretical potential of rejuvenating an entire human body back to a youthful state" (West, 2013).

- The very appropriately named Methuselah Foundation said in 2015 that the human body "has a structure that determines all aspects of its function, including its chance of falling apart any time soon, so if we can restore that structure—at the molecular and cellular level—then we will restore function too, so we will have comprehensively rejuvenated the body" (Isaacson, 2015).

- A look at the matter of who, exactly, will benefit if immortality is achieved by us, the human race. Will it be widely available to all of us? Or, will it solely be for the benefit of a global elite? Has the secret to everlasting life already been found, or perfected? Is it being jealously guarded by powerful figures in government, the military, and the intelligence community?

CHAPTER 1

The Longest Lived
Aliens of All

When one addresses the matter of ancient extraterrestrials, their interactions with the human species tens of thousands of years ago, and the matter of immortal lives, it is vital that one starts with the saga of the Anunnaki. Why? Because a solid case can be made that it was the Anunnaki who were directly responsible for introducing the concept of immortality to the early people of our planet, even if they were very careful not to share all of its secrets with too many of our species. Certainly, as we'll soon see, although immortality may have been a routine state of body and mind for the Anunnaki, only a lucky, select few of humanity were genetically altered to such a degree that they could quite literally keep the grave at bay and, possibly, even to an almost unending degree. Those same, select few were some of the most well-known figures in the Bible—a story that is told very soon.

We are told of these death-defying beings from another, far-away world that in the history of the Sumerian culture the Anunnaki amounted to "good and evil gods and goddesses (duality) who came to Earth to create the human race. According to the some resources [*sic*], these gods came from Nibiru—'Planet of the Crossing'" ("Sumerian Gods and Goddesses—the Anunnaki," 2016)."

A great deal has been said and written about the humanoid, possibly even giant-sized, Anunnaki—much of it by the late Zecharia Sitchin, who graduated from the University of London and who, for many years, worked as a journalist in Israel. Sitchin was the author of more than a few books on the Anunnaki, the mysterious origins of the human race, and alien-human interaction at the dawning of civilization and, perhaps, much earlier too. He knew of what he wrote.

The Anunnaki were fearless gods; they were at times ruthless, and always imposing. On occasion, they come across not unlike spoiled, crazed brats; ones who would wreak havoc on our planet and in just about any callous fashion they saw fit. The Anunnaki dominated the lives and the belief system of the ancient people of what was once called Mesopotamia, but which, today, is referred to as the Tigris-Euphrates river system. Were they fearless? There is no doubt about that. Were they ruthless? Yes. Imposing? Always. But were they literal gods? That's the most controversial question of all in this particular saga.

Zecharia Sitchin thought no, they were not gods, even though they were widely perceived as such. His research took him in a very different direction to the one dominated by supernatural deities that dwelled in an afterlife-style realm. Having carefully studied and interpreted ancient cuneiform tablets referencing the presence and actions of the Anunnaki in Mesopotamia, Sitchin came to an astonishing and undeniably controversial conclusion. The Anunnaki were not gods, after all. Not even one, solitary god. Rather, they were an all-powerful extraterrestrial force that hailed from a faraway world called Nibiru. It was a planet which, Sitchin concluded, lurked in the far fringes of our Solar

System, and whose orbit brought it perilously close to the Earth every 3,500 years, or thereabouts. In doing so, the massive planet's gravitational pull provoked worldwide havoc and destruction on our world every few millennia—hence the reason why so many ancient texts exist that describe worldwide cataclysms thousands of years ago.

Genetic Manipulation, Nuclear War, and Gold

In my 2015 book, *Bloodline of the Gods*, I told the story of how, at least hundreds of thousands of years ago, the Anunnaki dispatched an absolute armada of craft to the Earth with one primary goal in mind. That goal was to plunder our planet of its valuable resources, and specifically its abundant, rich supply of gold. The Anunnaki, however, weren't going to do their own dirty work when they could have someone else do it for them. Using highly advanced technologies, medicine, and science, they chose to genetically alter primitive, proto-humans and turn them into a subservient and sterile slave race. They were almost certainly responsible for the Rh negative blood anomaly that, today, courses its way through the veins of a small number of the human race; many of whom, as I demonstrated in my book, are intimately linked to the UFO phenomenon, alien abductions, and close encounters.

In my follow-up book, 2016's *Weapons of the Gods*, I revealed how, in the early years of civilization in portions of Africa and the Middle East, the Anunnaki splintered to the point where faction turned upon faction and with a catastrophic outcome for both them and us. The result of this splintering was that Anunnaki violently fought Anunnaki on our planet with tactical nuclear weapons—something which led to the decimation of Sumer and the cities of Sodom and Gomorrah, and caused equally massive destruction in northern India, as graphically told and described in the pages of the Indian epic, the *Mahabharata*.

There is, however, a third component to the story of the Anunnaki; it's an important component that takes us down the path toward the domain of immortality. Before we get to the important issue of *how* exactly the Anunnaki achieved immortality, it is first vital that we are able to make a solid case to the effect that they *did* indeed manage to conquer death—as amazing as such a thing surely sounds.

Welcome to the Creation of the Human Race

According to both the old cuneiforms and Sitchin's interpretations, the very same Anunnaki personnel that arrived on our planet hundreds of thousands of years ago—spearheaded by Enki and Enlil, who were the sons of the Anunnaki overlord, Anu—were still very much alive, vibrant, and active up until several millennia prior to the birth of Jesus Christ. If that is true, then they clearly had life spans of a kind that we can scarcely even begin to comprehend. We are told that the Anunnaki were human-like to the extent that, eventually, they were able to successfully mate with humans. As a result, they created demi-god-like offspring. This is a sure sign that, just like us, the Anunnaki were born, lived, and died—at least, that is, until they managed to largely eradicate the final stage of life. Death, what else?

That the Anunnaki were experts in the field of genetic manipulation and its many and varied complexities is something that has been skillfully demonstrated by writer Joan d'Arc. She provides the following, which describes what specifically happened *after* the Anunnaki made those first adjustments to the early, proto-humans: "The Biblical story of the creation tells that man and woman were not created at the same time but, rather, the female was created (or as Sitchin translates, 'cloned') from the male. During this operation, as the Bible tells us, a 'rib' was removed from The Adam" (d'Arc, 2000); Adam being, of course, the first true man according to biblical texts.

Joan d'Arc continues that Sitchin's conclusion was that the rib was chosen for a specific reason. Or, maybe, it wasn't a rib that was extracted, after all. She notes that the process of cloning specifically requires the usage of what are termed the "least differentiated cells." Rather intriguingly, one can find these in the cells of the human stomach—the stomach, of course, being very close to the rib cage. Thus, perhaps, the story had to a degree been distorted with time to where cellular material became a rib, a story still faithfully embraced by millions to this very day. But this was not so for Sitchin, who was absolutely sure that the old tales were distortions of early, but highly advanced cloning techniques undertaken by immortal aliens (ibid.).

From Sitchin's perspective, whatever the true nature of the extraction of something from Adam—something which, whether indirectly or directly, led to the creation of Eve—it had to be connected to the reproductive system. This would, quite naturally, make a great deal of sense. We are talking about the compatibility of the egg and the sperm. That in much earlier times the Anunnaki had apparently, and quite deliberately, rendered their earlier slave race infertile strongly suggests that it may not have been a difficult task for them to have later reversed the process, thereby ensuring that the descendants of that same slave race finally had the ability to procreate and flourish— which is precisely what happened.

The Paradox of Why Even Immortals Can Die

Although the Anunnaki are said to have achieved life spans of in excess of 400,000 years—effectively rendering them near-immortal from our personal perspectives today—that doesn't mean they were not capable of dying. They most certainly were. The Anunnaki's incredible life spans were achieved by the very same things that, one day, might allow us to have incredibly long life spans: science, medicine, and technology. As Anunnaki expert Michael Sokolov says: "The ancient people indeed thought of their gods as immortal. They were not, however, immortal in the supernatural sense. They could be killed by accident or warfare, and radiation was just as deadly to them as it is to us" (Sokolov, 2016).

If the Anunnaki were careful and avoided death via the aforementioned accidents or warfare, says Sokolov, then their lives might very well have been potentially indefinite in length. Sokolov notes that when the Anunnaki waged war upon each other, and Egypt's Sinai Peninsula was devastated and ravaged by a series of tactical nuclear strikes of the types which I described in my *Weapons of the Gods* book, the Anunnaki ran for their lives. The reason they did so being the huge, ominous, and unstoppable radioactive clouds of death that were heading directly for them. Sokolov adds that Enki—who first traveled to the Earth close to half a million years ago, and who was still active on the planet up to around 4,000 years ago—did his utmost to try and save as many Anunnaki (and just about as many people) as possible from the deadly missiles and their attendant, radioactive terror.

Neil Freer has made thought-provoking observations on this particular issue, too. He states about the Anunnaki and their almost unbelievable longevity that they "did not give us the relatively extreme longevity or immortality they possessed by conscious deliberate decision. It did not fit their purposes: we were invented as slave workers. The records also show, however, that, over time, a handful of humans were granted immortality" (Freer, 2012). Those lucky souls were generally those who toiled hard for the Anunnaki and who were able to help keep the human populace in civilized states, something which the Anunnaki deeply approved of.

Now it's time to address the most important issue of all: *how* exactly the Anunnaki managed to achieve their much envied states of immortality. It's an issue of incredible proportions.

CHAPTER 2

Gold: The Key to Eternal Life

On the matter of how and under what specific circumstances the Anunnaki achieved what may very well have been full-blown immortality, we have to turn our attentions to the one thing, more than any other, which seemingly dominated the minds and lives of all the Anunnaki. That thing was gold. Zecharia Sitchin came to believe that the reasoning behind the Anunnaki program to massively mine the Earth for its gold supplies was very much self-serving. He was right: survival vs. death was the name of the game, as it is for just about every living creature.

Interestingly, the late Lloyd Pye, an investigator of the many and varied mysteries surrounding the origins of the human species, came to a near-identical, independent conclusion to that of Sitchin. Pye said that Sumerians "left detailed written accounts of how these off-world beings they called 'Anunnaki' came down from the heavens to live among them as overlords . . . The Sumerians claim this information was given to them by their multiple 'gods,' the Anunnaki, which is one of many strong supports for the truth of their account" (Pye, 2011).

There was something else, too, when it came to the matter of the Anunnaki. In essence, both Sitchin and Pye believed that the mining of gold was undertaken to save not just the Anunnaki themselves, but also their alleged home world, Nibiru.

Racing to Save a Planet

Sitchin and Pye concluded that despite the incredible sciences and infinitely advanced technologies in their possession, the Anunnaki were far from being infallible. They were deeply afraid of something that threatened their very existence: namely, the destruction of their huge, distant home world. Not in the sense that Nibiru would be *literally* destroyed, but rather, that its atmosphere—already degrading to a dangerous degree—would collapse, and to such an extent that their planet would be rendered largely uninhabitable. Imagine a situation not unlike our own concerns about holes in the ozone layer, but multiplied countless times over. That is what the Anunnaki are said to have been faced with. So, how could such a disastrous situation be averted permanently? By the use of gold, that's how.

It's notable that by interpreting ancient texts, legends, and the beliefs of the Sumerians, both Pye and Sitchin came to believe that the Anunnaki were taking massive amounts of gold from the Earth, reducing it down to a fine powder, and then flooding incredible amounts of powdered gold into Nibiru's atmosphere to, essentially, plug the holes that threatened to destroy the atmosphere and the entire Anunnaki civilization, too. If such a thing sounds like over-the-top science-fiction, it's actually not. Science-*fact* is very much the order of the day.

In the early 1970s, when concerns about our very own ozone layer grew, Dr. Edward Teller, a brilliant physicist and someone with deep links to the world of official secrecy, theorized that millions of tons of terrestrial gold dust, launched into space on numerous cargo-craft, could effectively be used to fix the problems with the ozone layer. It was an ingenious theory. So far, it has not been put into action. At least, not by us it hasn't. But, just maybe, someone else—the Anunnaki, perhaps—attempted and even succeeded in achieving something nearly identical, albeit hundreds of thousands of years ago. Let's hope that our recklessness when it comes to the environment doesn't force us to go down that very same path.

Such talk, of utilizing certain elements to save our atmosphere—and, potentially, every living thing on the planet—was the subject of great debate in the latter part of 2009. That was when the United States' House Select Committee on Energy Independence and Global Warming got in on the debate. Dr. John P. Holdren, science adviser to the White House, came up with a potential plan that was nearly identical to that of Dr. Edward Teller, and even to the program of the Anunnaki.

The big question provoked by all this is: what does all of this have to do with extraterrestrial immortality? The answer is an intriguing one; it lies in a *second*, gold-based program, one that each and every one of the Anunnaki relied upon for their ongoing existences and their unending life spans. In that sense, gold played a dual role in the world of the Anunnaki: it saved their planet from destruction, and it saved the Anunnaki themselves from irreversible, physical death.

The Answer to Immortality

Of the many mysterious issues presented in this book, certainly very near the top of the list, is that surrounding what has become known as White Powder Gold and, alternately, as high-spin monatomic gold powder. It is, reportedly, a life-extending substance of an almost magical nature, one which the Anunnaki craved and relied upon. Its secrets and potentials lead us in the direction of the mysterious art of alchemy—much of which is devoted to uncovering the secrets of the so-called Philosopher's Stone. It is a strange and enigmatic substance which, in essence, is a catalyst allowing base metals to transform into gold. The Philosopher's Stone can supposedly do much more than that. It is also referred to as the Elixir of Life, which, in a liquid gold form, will provide the imbiber with an everlasting existence, as it did for the Anunnaki.

Kitty Bishop, PhD, says that this life-giving substance runs like a "red thread which weaves through the life stories of the prophet Enoch [who, as we shall soon see, is said to have reached the very enviable age of 365], Thoth (the Egyptian God of the Moon, Magic and Writing) and Hermes Trismegistus, all of whom are reported to have consumed 'the white drops' or the 'white powder of gold' as the elixir was called— thereby achieving immortality" (K. Bishop, 2010).

Trismegistus, for those who may be wondering, is said to have been the author of the *Hermetic Corpus*, priceless texts penned between the second and third centuries AD. It's thought-provoking to note that, for the people of ancient Greece, Enoch and Trismegistus were perceived as being one and the same. Trismegistus penned the *Emerald Tablets of Thoth*. It's a portion of the ancient Greek texts known as the *Hermetica* and which focuses on alchemy and the Elixir of Life (ibid.). Thus, we see a notable and eye-opening thread developing.

On the matter of Thoth, back in 1928 Manly P. Hall, a prolific author and mystic, wrote the following words:

> While Hermes still walked the earth with men, he entrusted to his chosen successors the sacred *Book of Thoth*. This work contained the secret processes by which the regeneration of humanity was to be accomplished and also served as the key to his other writings. Nothing definite is known concerning the contents of the *Book of Thoth* other than that its pages were covered with strange hieroglyphic figures and symbols, which gave to those acquainted with their use unlimited power over

the spirits of the air and the subterranean divinities. When certain areas of the brain are stimulated by the secret processes of the Mysteries, the consciousness of man is extended and he is permitted to behold the Immortals and enter into the presence of the superior gods. The *Book of Thoth* described the method whereby this stimulation was accomplished. *In truth, therefore, it was the "Key to Immortality* [italics mine]" (Hall, 2010).

So, we have several, key issues in this expanding story. They are issues that encompass alchemy, mysterious white droplets, powdered gold, a man—Enoch—who lived for hundreds of years, and the answer to immortality. Now, we'll see precisely why and how we have those threads and what they mean and offer.

From Nibiru to Marrs

Jim Marrs is right on the money when he says that, in recent years, White Powder Gold, the mysteries of alchemy, and extensive life spans have all intrigued some of the finest minds and experts on such matters. Marrs has suggested that there is a connection between the curious powdered gold and the Manna of the Bible, as well as to the mysterious so-called Bread of Presence, which played such a major role in Egyptian history and lore. Of equal importance are the worlds of the late Laurence Gardner. He, too, was someone who extensively pursued the mysteries surrounding the Anunnaki and their immortal lives.

Gardner's extensive work accorded very closely to that of Sitchin; particularly so when it came to the matter of the Anunnaki. Admittedly, Gardner did differ on a few issues, however; one of them being that of the age to which the Anunnaki typically lived. Whereas Sitchin was content to suggest in excess of 400,000 years, Gardner was more inclined to believe the figure was closer to 50,000 years—which is still an incredible and highly enviable life span, and practically an immortal life span from our personal perspectives.

On the matter of the ages of the Anunnaki, the Library of Halexandria makes a very intriguing statement. Conceding that Gardner and Sitchin weren't in accord when it came to ages and life spans, and regardless of the specifics of the life spans of the Anunnaki, the library notes it has been suggested that "the human life span, while enormously brief as compared to the Anunnaki gods and goddesses, might nevertheless be compensated by the humans possessing the ability to achieve a great deal in a relatively short time" ("Anunnaki," 2009).

Laurence Gardner astutely recognized that the ancients had a far greater awareness of this life-extending substance than we do today: "They knew there were superconductors inherent in the human body. They knew that both the physical body and the light body had to be fed to increase hormonal production and the ultimate food for the latter called shem-an-na by the Babylonians, mfkzt by the Egyptians and manna by the Israelites" (Gardner, 2016).

Gardner made a very interesting observation when he suggested that the tale of the ancient Greek quest to locate the elusive and legendary Golden Fleece was prompted by a desire—a pressing need, perhaps—to understand "the secret of this substance." Gardner made similar observations about the mysterious Ark of the Covenant or, to use an alternative term, the *golden* coffer. The secrets of gold completely dominated the quests, Gardner maintained, and with very good reason, too: to carefully and constantly avoid death (ibid.).

Without doubt, the most notable observation Gardner made on this issue revolved around an account that appears in Exodus 32:2 in the pages of the Old Testament. It is a very thought-provoking account that tells of how, while Moses was on the mountain communing with God, the Israelites melted down their many items of gold and turned them into a false god, a golden calf. Not only did this outrage both God and Moses, it also provoked the latter to do something very unusual, but decidedly intriguing, as Exodus makes very clear. That something mirrors what, today, we know about the Anunnaki and immortality.

Ingesting Gold Powder in the Old Testament

According to the relevant text from Exodus 32:2, it was while Moses was deep in communication with God—or, perhaps, with an important representative of the Anunnaki—that Aaron, the elder brother of Moses, became extremely frustrated by what he perceived as a lack of action and activity, particularly as a result of the fact that Moses was gone for such a long period of time and provided not even a smidgen of information regarding his activities. The result was that the Israelites became more and more angered about the situation and chose to take things into their own hands. That effectively meant denouncing God and creating brand-new deities. It was something, as we shall soon see, that did not sit at all well with the Anunnaki. Aaron ordered each and every Israelite to hand over every piece of gold they possessed. They did as they were told in rapid-fire fashion. The gold was then melted down by Aaron, who proceeded to fashion it into the form of a calf. It was a golden calf that doubled as a new god—at least, in the eyes of

The adoration of the golden calf (Hortus Deliciarum, 1180, Wikimedia Commons).

the Israelites it did. But Aaron didn't stop there. He soon crossed the proverbial line.

With a new god now firmly in place, Aaron created an altar to his god-like golden calf, at the foot of which the Israelites were told to pray. This was no sedate, quiet, church-like prayer meeting, however. Sacrificial offerings were made to the golden calf and a great deal of food was eaten, alcohol was downed, and wild, sexual antics followed. It was their equivalent of today's sex, drugs, and rock and roll.

Evidently, a faction of the Anunnaki was carefully and secretly watching this state of affairs and was far from happy with the situation. Outraged and furious would be far better terms to use. Word soon got back to Moses, who was still communing with his God in the mountains, that all was not well in the Israelite camp, not in the slightest. It was at this point that Moses was sternly ordered to return to the camp and get his people under control quickly or else. Exhibiting not just anger, but also a nearly deranged state of jealousy, God—or an Anunnaki representative—informed Moses of the creation of the golden calf and how the people were now worshiping it as nothing less than a god. Indeed, the voice from the heavens told Moses that it was all but ready to obliterate the Israelites from the face of the planet.

Moses, deeply concerned by this anger-filled, homicidal threat, begged God to reconsider; after all, it was God's work that had allowed the Israelites to leave Egypt behind them and start new lives in new places. For Moses, it made no sense to have come this far, only to bring it all to a destructive and fiery end, even if the Israelites had recklessly bowed down to a new god in his absence. Evidently, God didn't just listen to Moses; he listened very carefully and to the point where he agreed to give the Israelites a second chance—providing, that is, that Moses could get his people firmly inline. And, of course, there was the matter of that golden calf, which God was adamant had to go, again, or else.

The result was that Moses headed back down the mountain and made his way to the Israelite camp armed with that now famous pair of stone tablets, upon which were inscribed what are universally known as the Ten Commandments. The engravings, we are told, were the work of God himself. Although Moses was relieved that God had second thoughts about exterminating the Israelites, his relief was quickly turned to frustration and anger when he saw the people cavorting, engaging in orgies, and getting wasted—and all before the false god, the golden calf. So angry was Moses that he threw the tablets onto the ground and smashed them to pieces in the process. Then he did something very unusual, but also something very intriguing and which has a direct connection to the matter of immortality. So the story went, Moses seized the golden calf, burned and melted it within a powerful fire, and then ground it into a fine powder. That same powder was then mixed with water and was duly drunk by the Israelites, one and all.

Laurence Gardner noted the importance of this particularly important account that, for years, has puzzled theologians, "because heating or burning gold with fire does not, of course, produce powder; it produces molten gold. Later in the story, however, it is explained that the fine powder could be wiped with frankincense and made into bread cakes, which the old Septuagint Bible calls 'bread of the presence'" ("Monatomic Gold," 2006).

None of this was lost on Jim Marrs, either. He said, with a high degree of logic, that chugging down on a liquid cocktail—the primary content of which was gold—would not just be reckless or dangerous, it would prove to be downright deadly to one and all. Marrs did not, however, suggest that we should relegate the story to the domains of folklore and mythology. Instead, he believed—and made a very good case—that what was actually being described was a distorted story of the creation of immortality-giving White Powder Gold, or what is also termed High-Spin Monatomic Gold Powder.

And what, exactly, might that be? It's very probably the key, and the much sought-after answer, to how one may live forever. The Anunnaki clearly made massive use of it. Moses appeared to be fully aware of its incredible powers, too, even if his linkage to it has been distorted through the course of several millennia. All of which brings us to the mysterious world of a man named David Hudson.

The Strange Saga of "Orbitally Rearranged Mono-Atomic Elements"

More than four decades ago, David Hudson, an Arizona-based farmer whose income was derived from cotton, developed a keen interest in what is now known as the aforementioned Monatomic Gold Powder, or the aforementioned White Powder Gold. Although Hudson worked in the field of farming, he was someone who spent a great deal of his spare time focusing on something central to the theme of alien immortality. As his work and research progressed, Hudson gave a name to the mystery he uncovered and, finally, understood. He termed it Orbitally Rearranged Mono-Atomic Elements, or ORME, which also just happens to be the ancient Hebrew term for nothing less than The Tree of Life, which is just about the most appropriate and relevant terminology of all.

Many of Hudson's investigations led him down a pathway toward the mysteries of the atom, and to very surprising results concerning what is termed nucleus deformation. In simple terminology, during such deformation the nuclei—the core—of monatomic matter performed in a decidedly strange fashion and its configuration were altered. Hudson found that this specifically occurred in what are termed precious metals. Within this particular class are silver, palladium, rhodium, ruthenium, osmium, iridium, platinum . . . *and gold*. Dan Sewell Ward says of this issue: "Within the new configuration, the atoms interact in two dimensions, with the super-deformed nuclei reaching high spin, low energy states. In this state the elements become perfect superconductors, with their electrons combining in 'Cooper Pairs' and thus becoming photons of light" (Ward, 2003).

Jim Marrs notes the most eye-opening aspect of this issue: "When reaching this state, the electrons turn to pure white light, and the individual atoms separate, producing *a white monatomic powder* [italics mine]" (Marrs, 2013).

Ward says that a careful study of all the data, ranging from the scientific to the folkloric, suggests Hudson tapped into something that has the ability to utterly transform the human body, making amazing and positive changes to DNA, reversing the ravages caused by the likes of cancer and other potentially fatal conditions, and even leading us toward the door marked *Immortality*.

Ward is absolutely correct. A great deal of research—highly successful research, it is important to stress—has been undertaken and demonstrates that healing the body with gold is not as unlikely as it does undeniably sound. In fact, it works only too well. Orogoldschool.com states that "scientists now believe that they may have found a way to utilize gold and nanotechnology together, and may be able to treat cancer without any of the severe side effects" ("Precious Metals in Medicine—How Gold Can Treat Cancer," 2016).

Gold and Cancer

At the forefront of this undeniably groundbreaking work is the staff of Rice University, Texas. Personnel at the university have seen great and astonishing success when those afflicted with cancer are injected with small spheres wrapped in gold. Nanoparticles exit the bloodstream and focus all of their attention upon the cancerous tumor. Infra-red light is then "blasted" onto the tumor, something that allows the gold's nanoparticles to change the light into heat and effectively cause the obliteration of the tumor.

In a June 1, 2014, press release, Rice University explained that its work demonstrated the process would kill off cells that were cancerous, but would not harm non-cancerous cells or organs—which is one of the unfortunate side effects of more conventional ways of trying to combat cancer. In fact, it was reported that Rice's methods had proved to be around 17 times more successful than those procedures that relied upon regular chemotherapy-based treatment, and particularly so regarding cancers in the head and the neck.

Rice University staff continue that one particular "component" in the process of defeating cancer involves "an injectable solution of non-toxic gold colloids, tiny spheres of gold that are thousands of times smaller than a living cell. Quadrapeutics represents a new use of colloidal gold" (Boyd, 2014).

The Importance of the ORME

Things get even more controversial: it was Hudson's conclusion that when the powdered gold is ingested—in Orbitally Rearranged Mono-Atomic Element (ORME) form—a person is essentially transformed into a new being, one that possesses the skills of biolocation (divining), levitation, telepathy, having the ability to influence the minds of others, and even bringing new life into the recently dead. The latter being something the Anunnaki were allegedly highly adept at achieving.

It should be noted there are other, somewhat different, views concerning White Powder Gold, which brings us to the work of Anna Hayes. She says that this life-giving substance briefly fires up "the dormant codes in the higher dimensional DNA strand Templates, releasing bursts of higher frequency into the DNA template, creating temporary 'windows' to the higher dimensions and giving the physical body a temporary boost" (Hayes, 2000).

Clearly, then, there are many questions concerning, and mysteries surrounding, the matter of High-Spin Monatomic Gold Powder. Could one day the mysteries of gold allow us, the human race, to open the door to immortality, in much the same way as it did for the Anunnaki, and who knows how long ago? Very possibly, yes. In fact, as we'll see in a later chapter, a top secret, clandestine attempt to uncover the truths of immortality may have taken place when the 2003 invasion of Iraq kicked off. Taking out Saddam Hussein and his cronies may not have been the only motivation for going to war. It may have literally been a matter of life and death. For the victor: unending life and zero death.

CHAPTER 3

Methuselah, the Oldest Man on Earth

Of all the characters who appear in the pages of the Bible, and specifically in the Old Testament, one of the most intriguing and mysterious of all is Methuselah. He was the grandfather of none other than Noah, of both flood and ark fame. Methuselah was not only a part of a lineage that led from Adam and Eve to Noah and, ultimately, to Jesus Christ himself, he also had the distinction of reportedly being the longest-lived human in recorded history. Period. Methuselah allegedly had a life span of, rather incredibly, 969 years—*almost one full millennium*. Not only that, the story that surrounds Methuselah is filled with tales that can easily be placed in an extraterrestrial context. It is also a story that is dominated by tales of strange and unearthly offspring, journeys into what sounds distinctly like outer space, and numerous characters with massive longevity.

To have an understanding of who precisely Methuselah was, we have to turn our attentions in the direction of the Old Testament; specifically to Genesis 5. In its pages we are told that when God brought the human race into being, he chose to make it in his very own image and specifically coined the term "mankind." From there, we're then given the lowdown on what many might perceive as the most important family in recorded history.

"So All the Days of Methuselah Were Nine Hundred and Sixty-Nine Years, and He Died"

Genesis 5 continues that at the ripe old age of no less than 130, Adam had a son. His name was Seth. As it turns out, however, Adam was still very much in his youth, as strange as that surely sounds to us. He is said to have lived for another 800 years after Seth's birth, thus making Adam 930 at the time of his death. Seth too, we are told, had an extraordinarily long life. He became a father to Enosh at 105. And Seth had many more years in front of him, too, reaching a very impressive 912. Following directly in his father's footsteps, at the age of 90 Enosh fathered Kenan and lived to the age of 905. Kenan pretty much did likewise: he became a father at 70 to Mahalalel and passed away at 910. Mahalalel lived for 895 years, while his son, Jared, reached a mind-boggling 962. Jared was the father to, among others, Enoch. Now it's time to take a look at the life of Methuselah.

Profiling the Oldest Man of All

Genesis 5 then tells us that at the age of 65—when most people are ready to retire and take things easy—Enoch fathered Methuselah. There was no slowing down for Enoch, however. The Old Testament says that Enoch lived for another three centuries, suggesting his overall life span was around 350 years. All of which brings us to the old phrase: like father, like son. Only a handful of years before he reached the age of 200, Methuselah had a child. His name was Lamech. As for Methuselah, he made it all the way to the age of 969, only three decades or so short of *one thousand years*, thus making Methuselah the oldest figure in the pages of the Bible and in the history of the human race.

Lamech was no slouch either when it came to the matter of having a son at an extraordinary age. He is said to have become a father at the age of 182. Lamech's son was one of the most famous of all the many and varied biblical characters: Noah. Lamech wasn't destined to have a life as long as that of his legendary father, however: he "only" reached 777—an age most of us would be more than happy to reach, providing we were able to retain a state of eternal youth. Noah followed the family trait for long lives: he made it to 950. His children were Ham, Shem, and Japheth.

Although the amount of background data on Methuselah is admittedly sorely limited, the Old Testament does provide us with at least a degree of background data. Indeed, further data on Methuselah can be found in the Bible, which provides us with a fair degree of insight into the man's life. By all accounts, he was a law-abiding, deeply religious individual; he was a man whose life was dictated by the word of God. He was someone who was careful to ensure that those with whom he came into contact knew of his ways and beliefs. Methuselah was also someone who taught people to follow the word of God, and not be swayed by false gods. The fear of God was something that was very often on the mind of Methuselah.

And, it must be said, the murderous actions of God—or of the Anunnaki—are extensively chronicled in the old book. As the Old Testament also reveals, however, the time came when the people fell off the straight and narrow so to speak and turned against God and his word. Methuselah, deeply concerned by this potentially dangerous situation, did his utmost to try and rectify things and implored people to come back to the path of his creator. It was, however, to very little avail. And when the people even turned on Methuselah, God ensured terrible harvests for those who turned away from him, something that provoked starvation and death.

There is a general acceptance among biblical experts that Methuselah died during the massive flood that dominates the story of Noah—something that suggests that had Methuselah *not* died as a result of the massive deluge that destroyed much of humankind, then he might have achieved an even greater age, possibly even surpassing 1,000. After all, he was only 31 years short of one millennium when the flood is said to have taken his life. It should also be noted that the Book of Luke, in the New Testament, offers a direct lineage from Adam, Enosh, Enoch, Methuselah, and the rest of the family, right up to Jesus. So, what we have here is an elite group of ancient humans, upon whom was bestowed the closest thing that we, today, could interpret as immortality—given our measly 80 or so years.

But were they really just humans who had incredible life spans? Or, was something else afoot?

Heading to the Heavens

It's very important to stress that Methuselah's father was Enoch. Why? Very simple: the Book of Enoch—a Jewish text that dates back to around 300 BC, but which clearly describes events that occurred much earlier, and which specifically did *not* make it into the pages of the Bible—tells an incredible story. It sounds like a story of a fantastic trip into outer space. By whom? By no one less a character than Enoch himself—the father of Methuselah, allegedly the oldest man ever to have walked the planet. The first portion of the Book of Enoch provides the following, in Enoch's own words, describing a flight with a band of what were described as angels. According to Enoch, in a translation prepared and provided by R.H. Charles in 1912:

"They took [and] brought me to a place in which those who were there were like flaming fire, and, when they wished, they appeared as men. And they brought me to the place of darkness, and to a mountain the point of whose summit reached to heaven. I saw the treasuries of all the winds: I saw how He had furnished with them the whole creation and the firm foundations of the earth. And I saw the corner-stone of the earth: I saw the four winds which bear the firmament of the heaven. And I saw how the winds stretch out the vaults of heaven, and have their station between heaven and earth: these are the pillars of heaven. I saw the winds of heaven which turn and bring the circumference of the sun and all the stars to their setting" (Charles, 1912).

Enoch continued:

"I proceeded to where things were chaotic. And I saw there something horrible: I saw neither a heaven above nor a firmly founded earth, but a place chaotic and horrible. And there I saw seven stars of the heaven bound together in it, like great mountains and burning with fire. Then I said: 'For what sin are they bound, and on what account have they been cast in hither?' Then said Uriel, one of the holy angels, who was with me, and was chief over them, and said: 'Enoch, why dost thou ask, and why art thou eager for the truth? These are of the number of the stars, which have transgressed the commandment of the Lord, and are bound here till ten thousand years, the time entailed by their sins, are consummated'" (ibid.).

Enoch added that he was then taken to what he described as yet another realm, one that was far more terrifying than anywhere else to which he had been exposed. It was nothing less than a fiery, flaming world, filled with dark and disturbing imagery of a hellish nature and appearance. So the story went, Enoch was told by an angel named

Uriel that the place that had plunged Enoch into a state of deep terror was none other than the prison of the angels—a place of incarceration from which none were ever destined to leave. Rather notably, ancient extraterrestrial researchers have suggested that the prison might not have actually been one that kept angels under lock and key, but those Anunnaki who had had sex with human women, which was perceived as a major transgression by the ruling elite of the Anunnaki.

"Mankind Worshipped the Watchers as Gods"

Peter R. Farley, who has made a very careful study of the Book of Enoch—which, I should stress, runs to far more than the extracts just referenced—suggests that Enoch was describing a flight into outer space with what, today, we would most likely call ancient extraterrestrials. At one point in the story, Enoch informs Methuselah that the angels took him to what is termed First Heaven, where he saw a huge body of water. Farley interprets this sea as being the Persian Gulf; seen as an amazed Enoch traveled through the skies above and looked down on the world far below him. A Second Heaven encountered by Enoch, Farley suggests, was a pulverized portion of the Earth's landscape—very possibly provoked by the Anunnaki's atomic wars, which led to the destruction of the likes of Sodom and Gomorrah. A reference made by Enoch to Paradise and the Tree of Life, Farley has suggested, was possibly an aerial viewing by him of the jungles of Africa.

Of what is described as the Fourth Heaven, Farley says that this was where Enoch was shown imagery of such heavenly bodies as the stars, and our very own Sun and Moon. Of course, from the perspective of Enoch, he could only rationalize what he was seeing from a religious rather than a scientific perspective. Farley says that the Fifth Heaven was the end of Heaven and Earth and the banishment place of "the angels who have connected themselves with women" and where he was able to "see seven stars of heaven bound together." Interestingly,

Farley suggests that these seven bound stars may actually have been a vast, orbiting, Anunnaki-created space station (Farley, 2016).

It should be noted that Farley is not alone in suggesting that Methuselah's father had a connection to extraterrestrials. The late Philip Coppens believed that the Book of Enoch tells us a great deal about alien visitations in the very distant past, providing that we interpret its contents in a certain, specific fashion, of course. Much of Coppens' work in this field revolved around the so-called Watchers.

As Coppens said, the Watchers made their first appearance in Sumer—a place inextricably tied to the matter of the Anunnaki and their presence on, and manipulation of, the Earth. According to Coppens, Sumer (or Shumer) translates as Land of the Watchers. Coppens was someone who took his inspiration on the matter of the Watchers from the Anunnaki-related conclusions of Zecharia Sitchin. Coppens said that the Watchers were not supernatural deities; they were aliens. He offered the following: "Those who did land, either mated or genetically engineered Mankind into its present form. As a consequence, Mankind worshipped the Watchers as gods" (Coppens, 2016).

From Enoch to Alien Abductions

It transpires that one of the most well-known of all the many modern-day alien abductees, Betty Andreasson, described the small, grey, bug-eyed creatures that she encountered on many occasions not as aliens, but as the Watchers. In 1990, Ray Fowler's book, appropriately titled *The Watchers* and which chronicled Andreasson's experiences, was published. This potential connection between the Watchers of the past and those of the present prompted researcher Gregory Little to dig further into the matter of Andreasson's encounters. Little, after carefully studying Fowler's book, noted something striking. In relation to Sheol—a dark and foreboding domain of the dead described in the Hebrew Bible—it was said that the overlords were angelic beings with grey skin and who were very of short stature; very much like the alien Greys of alien abduction lore in general and of the Andreasson affair in particular.

As for Zecharia Sitchin himself, he recorded that the Book of Enoch extensively detailed "not only one but two celestial journeys: the first one to learn the heavenly secrets, return, and impart the acquired knowledge to his sons [which included Methuselah]. The second journey was one way only: Enoch did not return from it, and thus the biblical statement that Enoch was gone, for the Elohim [a Hebrew term meaning "deity"] had taken him" (Sitchin, 1998).

Or, perhaps, from our time-frame and perspective, "abducted" would be a far more appropriate word to use than "taken."

Noah: Not of this World?

Now, we come to what is almost certainly the most sinister part of the Book of Enoch. And "sinister" is not an exaggeration; it's right on target. It tells a near-nightmarish story of a very strange-looking baby who, it transpires, turns out to be none other than Noah himself. According to Enoch, "my son Methuselah took a wife for his son Lamech, and she became pregnant by him and bore a son" (Charles, 1912).

This son, Noah, was no normal newborn, however. Indeed, it's safe to say that young Noah comes across as definitively *non*-human, perhaps even *inhuman*. Enoch said of the child that his body was white—as in literally white. Oddly, however, he also described his son's skin as being as red as a rose. There is, of course, a conflict here. But whatever the reason for Enoch's curious words, there seems to be little doubt that, in terms of his skin, Noah did not look like a normal, regular child. Then there was the matter of Noah's hair. In the Book of Enoch, Noah's hair is described as being as white as white could be. Even stranger, Noah had a pair of eyes that shone in a near-glowing fashion. In light of Enoch's words, it's scarcely at all surprising that Lamech was plunged into a state of fear by the weird, physical appearance of his newly born son, who sounds somewhat like an albino, one with more than a liberal amount of alien genes. In fact, so terrified by young Noah's appearance was Lamech that he aired his suspicions that Noah was not his child, but that of the angels.

Before we get to the next stage in the story, let's take a brief detour into the world of albinism, Noah, and the issue of what the Anunnaki may really have looked like.

Are the Anunnaki Albinos?

That's a very important and thought-provoking question. It is a highly controversial question, too. It's one that we will now try and answer. MedlinePlus says that albinism results when "one of several genetic defects makes the body unable to produce or distribute melanin. These defects may be passed down (inherited) through families. The most severe form of albinism is called oculocutaneous albinism. People with this type of albinism have white or pink hair, skin, and iris color" ("Albinism," 2016).

In April 2014, and on the matter of Noah being an albino, Mark Sanderson, the chairman of the United Kingdom's Albinism Fellowship group, said: "It's fair to say some people believe he had albinism because of his visual distinctiveness and obvious characteristics, but who knows. I think the link is quite tenuous though others might disagree" (Rose, 2014).

Now, let's see what people who have studied this issue from an extraterrestrial perspective have to say about the physical appearance of the Anunnaki. The Website "Enki Speaks" says of the Anunnaki that they were around eight feet in height, closely resembled albinos, and had distinctly pale skin. The site quotes one A. Bordon as stating that the Anunnaki have "a sort of sweat on their skin like a film, hair snow-white like white wool, kinky. They are the Tall Whites who are our main ancestors. Some of them wear their hair shoulder-length, others close-cropped. Their eyes are red when they are not wearing almost black contact-like lenses" (Lessin, 2015).

In view of all of this, a case can be made that Noah was not affected by what, today, is known as albinism. But, instead, that he was part-Anunnaki, whose natural appearance just happened to closely mirror the appearance of a human albino. And, now, back to the story in hand.

Panic in the Family of Forever

According to Enoch, when word finally reached Methuselah of what was going down, Methuselah traveled long and far to be with his son and to see what was afoot. On reaching Lamech, Methuselah demanded to know what on Earth was wrong. Or, maybe, he should have asked what *off* Earth was wrong. Lamech proceeded to relate the whole, strange story, namely, that of Noah's weirdly colored skin, his brilliantly white hair, and, not to forget, his near-glowing eyes. And Lamech was careful to tell his (very) old man that he suspected young Noah was the offspring of the angels. Upon hearing all this, Methuselah wasted no time in speaking with his own father, Enoch.

One can almost see Methuselah racing, in downright panicky fashion, to splutter the words out to Enoch. Just like Lamech, Methuselah related the facts concerning Methuselah's unique physical appearance. There was also a discussion of certain, unsettling feelings within the family that a terrible event was soon to engulf the Earth. Enoch was quick to offer a reply. It was not the reply that Methuselah was hoping for. Enoch revealed his apparent knowledge of a looming, worldwide disaster—namely the planet-pummeling flood, in which Noah was destined to play such an integral role.

According to Enoch, as a result of the angels—in reality, the Anunnaki—coming down to Earth and engaging in sex with human women, strange and unearthly offspring that were part-human and part-extraterrestrial began to spring up all across the planet. They were none other than the legendary giants of the Bible. As a result of this transgression to beat all transgressions, said Enoch, God was about to purify the planet. He was ready to do so in a truly drastic and nightmarish fashion: namely, by wiping out the vast majority of the human race, cleansing the planet, and starting over again—and in a world where women and angels (or women and Anunnaki) would never again cross-breed. It was to be, said Enoch, a year-long deluge that would all but devastate the entire world. There was, however, more: weird-looking Noah was being groomed as someone destined to survive the flood—along with his family—and, effectively, to reignite the human race and create a new world. It was Enoch who came up with Noah's name, and it was Enoch who made it clear to Methuselah that the stakes were not just high, but stratospheric. The Lord, said Enoch, had told him of the chaos that was to come. And, indeed, the great flood soon followed.

"Sprung . . . from the Angels"

What all of the above tells us is that from the era of Adam onward—and, according to the Book of Luke, right up until the time of Jesus—there existed a multigenerational family that displayed one particular and almost unique trait. That trait was incredible longevity. The most obvious example, of course, was Methuselah. But the likes of Enosh, Mahalalel, and all of the rest were hardly far behind in terms of the amazing ages they reached before finally dying.

In addition to that, we have one member of the same family, Enoch, quite likely having taken trips into outer space with what may well have been elite figures within the Anunnaki. And we have Noah, whose physical appearance was seemingly not at all like the Church prefers to present it.

Right in the middle of all this we have Methuselah, who was the son of Enoch, Lamech's father, and Noah's grandfather. And having almost reached the age of 1,000, Methuselah was, by our standards today, practically immortal. That all of these characters had such ties and links—not to mention undeniably unique lives and odd, physical appearances—is strongly suggestive of a connection to ancient extraterrestrials; beings from the stars who had achieved immortality, and who shared the secrets of everlasting life with key, formative figures in the early years of religion, the Bible, and recorded history.

And, finally, on this aspect of the story, in a strange fashion Methuselah still lives on. At least, he does in name. Welcome to the Methuselah Foundation, whose staff state: "For us, tackling aging is really about changing assumptions regarding what is and isn't possible for human life, health, and happiness. We believe that aging as we currently know it is not inevitable ("About Methuselah," 2016).

Maybe, one day, our science will permit us to reach the incredible 969 years that Methuselah achieved. Or, possibly, we'll be reliant on the return of the Anunnaki for that.

CHAPTER 4

Gilgamesh and a Quest for an Eternal Existence

The late Zecharia Sitchin, who was beyond any shadow of doubt the most learned figure when it comes to the matter of the Anunnaki, and who and what they really were, said:

> Once upon a time the whole of Mankind lived in Paradise—satiated from eating the Fruit of Knowledge, but forbidden from reaching for the fruit of the Tree of Life. Then God, mistrusting his own creation, said to unnamed colleagues: The Adam, having eaten of the Tree of the Knowing, "has become one of us; what if he puts forth his hand and took also of the Tree of Life, and ate, and lived forever?" And to prevent that, God expelled Adam and Eve from the Garden of Eden. Man

has searched for that God-withheld immortality ever since (Sitchin, 2010).

Sitchin continued as follows:

But throughout the millennia, it has gone unnoticed that while in respect to the Tree of Knowing Yahweh Elohim stated that having eaten of it, "The Adam has become one of us"— no such "as one of us" is asserted in respect to living forever from the fruit of the Tree of Life. Was it because "Immortality" dangled before Mankind as a distinctive attribute of the gods, was no more than a grand illusion? If ever did someone try to find out, it was Gilgamesh, King of Uruk, son of Ninsun and Lugalbanda (ibid.).

An Epic Tale Unfolds

In early 2003, an astonishing and historic discovery was made in the heart of war-torn Iraq. It was, many quickly came to believe, nothing less than the final resting place of a legendary, long-dead king—one who ruled over the city of Uruk, from which the country of Iraq takes its name: the aforementioned Gilgamesh. He was a powerful figure and someone who played a direct role in the strange story that this book tells; namely, that of unending life and its connection to powerful and manipulative extraterrestrials who spent a great deal of time on our planet, millennia ago. Just about everything we know about this ancient ruler comes from the *Epic of Gilgamesh*. It's often, but quite incorrectly, described as being a book. In reality, however, the story of Gilgamesh was actually recorded on a series of clay tablets, more than 4,000 years ago.

Jorg Fassbinder, of the Munich, Germany-based Bavarian Department of Historical Monuments, was one of those who was directly involved in the groundbreaking discovery, which was made at a site through which the Euphrates River once ran. It was not just the tomb of Gilgamesh that Fassbinder believed his team had found, but also the remains of portions of the city of Uruk itself. Fassbinder, in an interview with the United Kingdom's BBC, said at the time when the story exploded across the Internet that he couldn't "say definitely" it was the old king's tomb. He added, however, that "it looks very similar to that described in the epic. We found just outside the city an area in the middle of the former Euphrates River the remains of such a building which could be interpreted as a burial" ("Gilgamesh tomb believed found," 2003).

The *Epic of Gilgamesh* tells of the mighty king, after death, having been buried in a tomb below the Euphrates River when it diverged, leaving the previously water-filled area dry. Today, there is still a high degree of controversy regarding whether or not the tomb in question really is that of Gilgamesh. The fact is, however, that the location is broadly correct, as is the timeframe in which the tomb was constructed. And, of course, the discovered remains of a long-gone city point strongly in the direction of Uruk itself. All of which brings us to the matter of how and why Gilgamesh came to be so inextricably tied to the issues of extraterrestrials and immortality.

Gilgamesh, Part-Human, Part-"God"

The story of Gilgamesh, of his life, his adventures, of his quest for immortality, and, ultimately, of his death are detailed in the form of an extensive poem, one which surfaced out of Mesopotamia millennia ago. By all accounts, Gilgamesh was as feared just about as he was revered. There was a very good reason for this: *he was not entirely human.* As we have seen already, a number of legendary figures from biblical times—such as Noah and Methuselah—came from an Anunnaki-driven lineage. Or, at the very least, they were exposed to the secrets of White Powder Gold, which provided them with incredible longevity. That was the case for Gilgamesh, too, as Zecharia Sitchin noted:

> Having been the son of the goddess Ninsun and the high priest of Uruk, Gilgamesh was considered not just a demigod but "two thirds divine." This, he asserted, entitled him to avoid the death of a mortal. Yes, his mother told him—but to attain our longevity you have to go to our planet, Nibiru (where one year equals 3,600 Earth-years). So Gilgamesh journeyed from Sumer (now southern Iraq) to "The Landing Place" in the Cedar Mountains where the rocket-ships of the gods were lofted (Sitchin, 2006).

Baalbek: the "Landing Place" of the Anunnaki (Library of Congress, date unknown, Wikimedia Commons).

The so-called landing place, Sitchin believed, was Baalbek. It is a town situated in the Beqqa Valley, Lebanon. From the perspective of historians and archaeologists, Baalbek is best known for what is termed its "Stone of the Pregnant Woman." It is an absolutely huge slab of stone that has a weight in excess of 1,000 tons. Incredibly, however, for all of its impressive appearance and size, the stone is dwarfed by two others: one around 1,250 tons and the other almost a whopping 1,700 tons.

Sitchin made his position on the Baalbek issue very clear: "The great stone platform was indeed the first Landing Place of the Anunnaki gods on Earth, built by them before they established a proper spaceport. It was the only structure that had survived the Flood, and was used by Enki and Enlil as the post-Diluvial headquarters for the reconstruction of the devastated Earth" (ibid.).

But what was it that brought Gilgamesh to Baalbek? That's a very good question. The answer is illuminating and it adds yet further data to what we know of the Anunnaki presence on Earth, thousands of years ago.

The World of the Giant King

According to the ancient tablets, Gilgamesh ensured that Uruk became a veritable metropolis: it was protected and surrounded by a massive wall of a type that would have Donald Trump practically drooling at the mouth. Huge, stepped towers, temples, and palaces were very much the order of the day. Those luxuries came at a great cost, though. It was only due to the fact that Gilgamesh was a definitive tyrant that Uruk became a city of renown. Thousands of men were plunged into a collective state of slavery, and each and every one of them was forced to haul the massive stone blocks that were used to construct the expansive city. Endless numbers of women became Gilgamesh's sex slaves.

And one and all bowed down before him, fearful of his power and strength. There was a very good and incredible reason for all this.

Not only was Gilgamesh part-human and part-Anunnaki, he is said to have stood at around 11 cubits. In our world of today, that would equate to a height of an astonishing *16 to 18 feet*. Gilgamesh was, then, one of the legendary giants that featured in so many ancient, religious texts—the most famous of all probably being Goliath, the Philistine soldier memorably slain by David, who went on to become the King of Israel, and whose story is told in the Old Testament's Book of Daniel.

It's no wonder that Gilgamesh was so feared: coming face to face with such an immense, towering figure would likely have plunged just about everyone into states of overwhelming terror. Things began to change, however, when the people of Uruk—both its inhabitants and its slaves—began to display a fair degree of understandable rebellion against the Goliath-like Gilgamesh. In other words, enough was finally enough. So the *Epic of Gilgamesh* goes, the citizens of Uruk pleaded with the gods—who we can suggest with a fair degree of certainty were the Anunnaki—to do something about this cruel, power-obsessed giant. They did exactly that. They reportedly created a massive, hair-covered wild-man of Bigfoot-like proportions to do battle with the king. The name of this monster was Enkidu. Interestingly, we're told that, in part, Enkidu was created out of human saliva. This may, perhaps, be a wild distortion of a real event in which Enkidu was the product of advanced genetics, cloning, and DNA manipulation.

The *Epic of Gilgamesh* says of Enkidu that he was a hair-covered humanoid. In contrast to modern-day enigmas like Bigfoot and the Abominable Snowman, however, Enkidu's hair flowed long. He was also described as a creature having an affinity with animals, such as cattle and gazelles, with whom he would eat and drink (*The Epic of Gilgamesh*, 2003).

The Build-Up to the Battle of the Giants

A creature of the wilderness, Enkidu was far more beast-like than he was human, to the extent that his friends were wild animals, and their cave- and forest-based abodes were his, too. In the story, however, everything changes when a prostitute named Shamhat—who may actually have been of Anunnaki blood—seduces Enkidu and introduces him to the world of sex. Shamhat was not a prostitute who worked for money, however. Quite the contrary: she viewed the sexual act as being akin to what we would term a fertility rite. On this matter, we have the following from the *Epic of Gilgamesh*:

> Shamhat loosened her undergarments, opened her legs and he took in her attractions.
>
> She did not pull away. She took wind of him, spread open her garments, and he lay upon her.
>
> She did for him, the primitive man, as women do. His lovemaking he lavished upon her. For six days and seven nights Enkidu was aroused and poured himself into Shamhat. When he was sated with her charms, he set his face towards the open country of his cattle. The gazelles saw Enkidu and scattered. The cattle of open country kept away from his body. For Enkidu had stripped; his body was too clean. His legs, which used to keep pace with his cattle, were at a standstill. Enkidu had been diminished, he could not run as before. Yet he had acquired judgment, had become wiser. He turned back, he sat at the harlot's feet. The harlot was looking at his expression, and he listened attentively to what the harlot said. The harlot spoke to him, to Enkidu (ibid).

Shamhat said: "You have become wise Enkidu, you have become like a god. Why should you roam open country with wild beasts? Come, let me take you into Uruk the Sheepfold, To the pure house, the dwelling of Anu and Ishtar, Where Gilgamesh is perfect in strength, And is like a wild bull, more powerful than any of the people" (ibid.).

Giant vs. Man-Beast

Not surprisingly, Enkidu quickly became enamored with Shamhat and his first experience of sex. His old friends, the animals of the woods, however, viewed his actions as unforgivable and they quickly and unanimously cast him out. It's while in the sole company of Shamhat that Enkidu learns of Gilgamesh and his iron-fisted rule over the people of Uruk. He quickly decides to do something about it. Enkidu makes his way to the city and, in no time at all, he and Gilgamesh are engaged in a violent, hand-to-hand battle chiefly because, when Enkidu first crosses paths with Gilgamesh, he finds him about to violently rape a newly married woman. Enkidu is determined to stop Gilgamesh and the fight duly begins. The sight of two mighty titans doing their utmost to destroy one another must have been a terrifying, imposing sight for one and all. The outcome, however, was not the expected one—namely, one giant slain and the other one the victor.

After hours of mortal combat, Gilgamesh finally becomes the winner. But rather than kill Enkidu, the king has, by now, developed a great deal of respect for the wild man. And as a direct result, the pair quickly become great friends. It's then that they decide to go on a wild, adventure-filled road trip, so to speak. It's a trek that takes them to the aforementioned Cedar Mountains which, Zecharia Sitchin concluded, was the home of the Anunnaki's primary space-port on Earth. While there, they slaughter by decapitation the guardian of the site, one Humbaba. He, too, is a giant and, notably, one of an incredibly advanced age—which is surely a matter of relevance and significance. It transpires that Humbaba's role as the guardian of the aliens' landing site was assigned by Enlil. As we saw in Chapter 1, Enlil was one of the primary figures in the story of the Anunnaki presence on Earth and that concerning the aliens' ability to extend the human life span, when it saw fit to do so.

It's when the pair end the life of yet another legendary character—the Bull of Heaven—that matters really come to a head. Also known as Gugalanna, the Bull of Heaven was a Mesopotamian god that was believed to have originated in the constellation of Taurus; a definitive extraterrestrial, one might justifiably say. Gugalanna was also the consort to the Queen of the Underworld, whose name was Ereshkigal, and who was controlled by Anu, the Lord of the Sky.

There is, however, more to come. When Ishtar, a Sumerian goddess of fertility, gives herself to Gilgamesh, he refuses her offer of sex. And as a result of these two killings, the outraged gods/Anunnaki take out their vengeance upon Enkidu and he is killed. The gods infect him with a deadly virus—which has shades of something akin to today's sophisticated biological warfare, perhaps—and his life is soon over.

Gilgamesh is devastated by the death of his new friend. But Enkidu's passing has another effect on the giant king. He becomes fearful of his very own mortality and deeply ponders upon the matter to the point of obsession. Yes, Gilgamesh was said to be semi-human and semi-deity in nature—a demigod, as such renowned people were termed back then. But the fact that Gilgamesh was not *pure* Anunnaki meant that immortality was not his even though, admittedly, his life span was said to be significantly longer than any normal human. So, in the wake of Enkidu's death, Gilgamesh, realizing that time is not on his side, heads off on a quest to find the key to living forever and before it's too late.

Seeking the Secrets of Immortality

One of those that Gilgamesh chased down—arguably the most important figure in his quest to keeping death at bay—was Utnapishtim. In the *Epic of Gilgamesh*, Utnapishtim is the equivalent of Christianity's

Noah in the Bible and an ancestor of Gilgamesh. The Anunnaki Enki—whose involvement in the matter of immortality has already been highlighted—warns Utnapishtim that a devastating flood is coming to engulf the planet and that human civilization is about to end in a terrible, cataclysmic fashion. There is only one way to survive the deadly deluge, says Enki, and that's to build a massive ship, *an ark*. It's known as the Preserver of Life and is filled with the "seed" of every animal. And not forgetting Utnapishtim's family, too, one and all aboard survive the planet-wide disaster, after which—and thanks to the gods—Utnapishtim and his wife are made immortal. Was it via the ingestion of far more than liberal amounts of White Powder Gold, perhaps? Yes, almost certainly. It's as a result of this incredible and generous gift—or an elixir from the stars—given to Utnapishtim that makes Gilgamesh determined to track down Utnapishtim and, hopefully, attain unending life for himself.

By now, and an untold number of years after the flood waters have receded, Utnapishtim is living with his wife on a remote island—an island that Gilgamesh is able to finally reach thanks to one Urshanabi, a man who holds the secrets that allow for passage across what are known as the Waters of Death. On finally reaching the island, Gilgamesh meets with Utnapishtim and the king opens up on his deep-seated fear of death. Though Utnapishtim is certainly not unsympathetic to Gilgamesh's anxieties, he makes it clear that only the gods can make man immortal. Man, himself, does not have the ability or the right to make man an entity that can keep death at bay on an unending basis. There is, however, still a small glimmer of hope for Gilgamesh.

As Gilgamesh prepares to leave the island, at the urging of Utnapishtim's wife he is told of a unique plant, one with near-magical properties and which can rejuvenate the human body. Utnapishtim chimes in and makes it clear that the plant does not ensure immortality, but only provides those who partake of it a second chance to be young again. The only problem: the plant is exclusively situated on the surrounding seabed. Nevertheless, in a highly unlikely fashion, Gilgamesh finds just such a plant by weighting heavy rocks to his feet and sinking to the ocean floor! This is according to the old legend, of course.

Overjoyed, and upon his return to the surface world, Gilgamesh says excitedly to the husband and wife who cannot die that he will head back to Uruk and feed some of the plant to "an ancient" and "put the plant to test." Disaster, however, is looming large: as Gilgamesh washes in the waters, a huge serpent lunges forward and steals the plant. Utterly crushed and defeated, Gilgamesh heads back to the city he rules over and finally resigns himself to a relatively short life. But, as it transpires, his life was not too short. According to the old texts, Gilgamesh was in power for close to 130 years. As for at what age, specifically, Gilgamesh may have attained the status of a king, that remains a mystery. Even so, if we suggest he was only 20 at the time he came to power, this would mean he lived for around 150 years—almost twice the life span of the average person today. It would seem, then, that being a demigod meant that Gilgamesh's DNA and genetic makeup were significantly different to those of the rest of the population in both approximately 2,500 BC and today, in the 21st century (ibid.).

It should be noted that much of the *Epic of Gilgamesh* is told in a highly fanciful, exaggerated, and distorted fashion. But when we remove ourselves from that same exaggeration and distortion, and instead address matters from a grounded, scientific perspective, what we see is this: thousands of years ago, King Gilgamesh, of the city of Uruk, knew something of how the immortal gods (or the everlasting Anunnaki) could bestow never-ending life on specific people of their choosing. History has shown that, despite his best efforts, Gilgamesh was not destined to be one of them, but he certainly came closer than most people of that era ever did.

2015: New Information Surfaces

In October 2015, a sensational discovery—directly relevant to the *Epic of Gilgamesh*—surfaced in Iraq, as Open Culture's Ted Mills revealed that "one of the oldest narratives in the world, got a surprise update last month when the Sulaymaniyah Museum in the Kurdistan region of Iraq announced that it had discovered 20 new lines of the Babylonian-Era poem of gods, mortals, and monsters" (Mills, 2015).

Mills noted that due to the fact that portions of the epic poem have been circulating since at least the 1700s, it's not at all surprising that further, related material might surface in the 21st century. Ironically, as Mills also revealed, it was hostilities—namely the 2003 war in Iraq—that provoked the finding of this new material, as a result of "the intense looting that followed," and which "yielded something new" (ibid.).

If never before seen material on the *Epic of Gilgamesh* and the characters contained within it can surface well into the second decade of the 21st century, then it's not at all out of the question that, one day, we may well learn even more about this mighty and enigmatic king including, perhaps, data that might provide amazing insight into the world of immortality and its extraterrestrial origins.

CHAPTER 5

Manna from the Skies

Now it's time to address the matter of yet another mysterious substance that nourished the ancients and which, rather intriguingly, is also said to have come from the skies above. In this case, quite literally, it rained down upon those chosen by God to receive it. It goes by the name of Manna, and it fed the Israelites for more than a few years—in fact, for no less than 40 of them. The story is told in the pages of Exodus 16, in the Old Testament. It describes under what specific circumstances the Israelites left slavery and bondage behind them, and how they came to be led by Moses to Mount Sinai with their planned, final destination being Canaan. It was otherwise known as the Promised Land, on account of the fact that God had deigned it so to Abraham, one of the Old Testament's three patriarchs; the others being Abraham's son, Isaac, and his grandson, Jacob.

Exodus tells us that the Israelites left Elim—which is believed to have been situated close to the east shore of the Red Sea—behind them and headed to the Desert of Sin, also referred to as the Wilderness of Sin. It should be noted that the title has nothing at all to do with sinning or sinners. Rather, it is a reference to an ancient Mesopotamian deity named Sin, who was the god of the Moon. Notably, Sin was the offspring of two of the most powerful figures in the story of the Anunnaki: Ninlil and Enlil. Thus, we see how inextricably tied to the world of the Anunnaki Moses and the Israelites really were.

Exodus makes it very clear that many within the Israelite community who had trusted Moses to keep them safe quickly turned their backs on the man, chiefly because as they made the trek from Elim to the Desert of Sin, food supplies became perilously scarce. What began as growing hunger soon bordered upon complete and utter starvation. Something had to be done, and done quickly, or widespread death was destined to be the only, inevitable outcome. Though it may have looked as if overwhelming starvation and grisly deaths were all but inevitable for the Israelites, such was not the case after all. God intervened. Or, perhaps, the Anunnaki did.

Food from the Gods

Evidently aware that the supplies of the Israelites were dwindling fast, and with nothing of any significance to replace it, the Almighty thundered to Moses that he would take charge of the situation and ensure that death by starvation would not occur. Moses was told by the all-powerful voice from above that bread would rain down from God's heavenly abode and, as a result, all would be good. Moses was instructed to tell his people to collect the nourishing food, and specifically just a sufficient amount for each day.

With relief, as well as an apparent abundance of food thankfully now looming on the horizon, Moses and Aaron told the Israelites that they would know it was God himself who had saved them from a life of slavery under the ruthless Egyptians, that it was God who had guided them through the desert landscape, and that it was God who—responding to the precarious state of affairs they now found themselves in—would save them from starvation and death. Moses then ordered Aaron to speak before the Israelites and instructed them to stand before God, who was now responding to their pleas for help. As they did so, and so Exodus reveals, God suddenly appeared before the quickly amazed throng of people. As Aaron continued with his speech, something incredible happened: across the desert plains, a mysterious cloud was seen by one and all, a cloud which reportedly contained the glory of God himself. Of course, one could make a logical case for the cloud being some sort of Anunnaki spacecraft hovering above the harsh, desert environment.

The voice of God boomed out of the cloud. Or, maybe far more likely, it was blasted out of a highly sophisticated Anunnaki equivalent of a powerful microphone or loudspeaker. The voice told the Israelites that they would not be left to starve and die. In fact, quite the opposite: they were told that at sunset they would receive a plentiful amount of meat, and at daybreak there would be an abundance of bread. The entity behind the voice then added, for good measure, that the Israelites—soon to be fed and saved—would know that he was the one and only true God and that they should bow down before him, and renounce any and all false gods.

It transpires that God proved good on his word. On the following morning, and as the Israelites awoke from their sleep, they found that a layer of dew had settled around their encampment. When, however, the dew evaporated, in its place was something else. It was a huge amount of unusual-looking flakes that resembled frost. One and all were utterly baffled, having never before seen anything like this curious, unique substance. Moses, however, knew exactly what it was. It was none other than the food of God, the promised bread that was destined to keep the Israelites from slow and torturous deaths due to starvation. Moses told the people to collect as much as was needed for each family or individual. God had made good on his promise and, in no time at all, the depressed spirits of the Israelites were suddenly transformed. There was finally light at the end of the dark tunnel after all.

The Manna Mystery

Exodus continues that the mass of people, now aware that they had been saved, dutifully followed Moses' words. There was no frantic grabbing of the curious food; everyone did as they had been told and collected whatever they needed, whether in large or small amounts. As a result, there was plenty to go around for everyone. There was, however, one specific and important stipulation: Moses was told by his God that all of the food must be eaten on the day it was collected; it must not be stored overnight and used the following day. Despite Moses' words—as delivered to him by God—some of the Israelites ignored Moses and chose to hoard the much-needed food in their tents. It was an action that proved to be costly: on waking the next day they found that the saved food was now rotten, stinking, and infested with maggots. A lesson was learned. The story continues that on each and every subsequent morning, the Israelites collected as much of the mysterious food as they could and ate it on that specific day, too.

According to the story, on the sixth day the Israelites collected double the previous amounts. There was a good reason for this: the following day was the Sabbath. So, they cooked the extra food 24 hours prior to the day of rest and stored it, specifically to avoid having to work on the Sabbath. Interestingly, on this occasion the food did not rot away as it had on previous days when kept for an extra day. In all probability this was nothing more than a carefully constructed tale designed to stress the importance of the Sabbath, the day of rest, and its associations to God.

That's, however, when problems began, as Exodus demonstrates. Despite having enough food for one and all, there were those within the Israelite camp who were still not satisfied with what had been provided to them by God/the Anunnaki. Despite being told that the Sabbath was to be a day of rest, some completely ignored the message and headed off to collect more of the mysterious food of God. Nevertheless, nothing was to be found and Moses had harsh words for those who had ignored his message. God chimed in, too, complaining in ominous tones about the rebellious nature of the Israelites and their determination to ignore the order to rest on the Sabbath. Not surprisingly, the thunderous voice soon ensured that everyone quickly towed the line.

It's at this point in the story that we finally get a solid description of this mysterious food. We also get a name for it, too. The bread-like substance was known to the Israelites as Manna. By all accounts, it was far from bland. In fact, it was said to be delicious, a sweet food made of wafer and tasting of honey. The story continues that God instructed Moses to tell Aaron to take a specific amount of Manna and to store it for future generations, specifically so that those same subsequent generations would know how God saved the Israelites from near-certain death.

Exodus then states that Aaron did as he was told, placing the nourishing Manna alongside the legendary tablets that displayed the Ten Commandments, which evidently pleased God. Indeed, so pleased was God that the Israelites received enough Manna to survive for a full four decades and they reached the land of Canaan. All of this begs a number of important questions: What, exactly, was Manna? How was it able to nourish the Israelites for 40 years? And how and why did it rain down from the skies above?

Manna: What Was It?

That Manna fell from the heavens—or perhaps, more correctly, was carefully and deliberately dropped from the skies—demonstrates that it was not a regular form of food. And clearly, because it didn't grow in the ground or fall from trees, the strong likelihood is that it was manufactured—but by whom? It's intriguing that God intervened to help the Israelites, lest they might starve to death as they crossed the harsh wasteland, and that the glory of the Lord appeared within the heart of what was described as a cloud. But was it really a cloud? Could it, actually, have been something else, such as a highly advanced aerial craft of the Anunnaki, one on an emergency mission to ensure that the Israelites did not die of starvation? We may never have a clear-cut answer to that question, but everything about this story smacks of direct ET intervention undertaken in a fashion similar to today's United Nations-based relief operations in parts of the world where a lack of both food and water are everyday hazards.

The *Catholic Encyclopedia* notes of Manna: "The name is connected with the exclamation 'Man hu,' which the Israelites uttered on first seeing it. This expression since the time of the Septuagint is generally translated 'What is this?' though it should more probably be translated 'Is this manna?' or 'It is manna'" (Knight, 2012). Not without significance—and surely not coincidental—is the fact that within ancient Egypt there was a foodstuff known as Mannu. The deep similarities between the words Manna and Mannu strongly suggests a direct connection. Maybe, they were one and the same.

The *Catholic Encyclopedia* has also noted that a number of biblical experts who have studied the matter of Manna have suggested it may actually have been a form of juice that can be extracted from Tamarix gallica, which is a form of shrub found in the vicinity of the Sinai Peninsula and Saudi Arabia. It stands to a height of around 15 feet. The juice in question was known by the locals, millennia ago, as Mann Es-Sama, which translates as a heavenly gift. No wonder, then, that suggestions have been made that Manna and Mann Es-Sama were one and the same. There is, however, a problem with this scenario. The biblical Manna, as we have seen, very quickly degraded, rotted, and attracted maggots. Mann Es-Sama does not degrade and retains its original state for extensive periods of time. Nor can it be made into a form of bread or cake.

It should also be noted that the juice in question, which can indeed be extracted from the Tamarix gallica shrub, is nearly 100 percent sugar, which, of course, creates a big problem when it comes to suggesting it nourished the Israelites for 40 years. No one could live on nothing but a sugary substance for 40 years, even if it was very occasionally supplemented by meat and other food items of a regular nature. There is also the not insignificant fact that to feed the massive numbers of Israelites for four decades, the supply must have reached incredible proportions. This, too, is suggestive of an ongoing relief effort, with Manna being shipped out to Moses and his people on a regular basis and via that mysterious cloud.

Another candidate that has been suggested for Manna is a certain lichen: Lenora esculenta, which can be found in North Africa. It is often carried by powerful winds and, as a result, falls to Earth. The people of North Africa have long used Lenora esculenta as a food source, specifically in the form of a type of bread. The problem, however, is that although it will certainly keep hunger away during times of starvation and strife, in the long term it poses more problems than it alleviates and for one, chief reason: it lacks any kind of nutrients. In other words, it fills the stomach but offers practically nothing at all of a health-supporting nature. Clearly, this is not a substance that would have kept the Israelites fit, robust, and healthy for a period of around four decades. The mystery of Manna, then, remains. Or does it?

Jim Marrs has suggested a connection between Manna and the food of the Anunnaki: White Powder Gold. Marrs states that the late Laurence Gardner—an authority on the Anunnaki—observed that the world's most ancient, acknowledged complete manuscript, which is known as the Egyptian *Book of the Dead*, speaks of the Egyptian kings and queens eating what is termed the Bread of Presence, and "while making the ritualistic journey to the afterlife" (Marrs, 2013). So, we have a Manna-like substance in Egypt linked to immortality in the afterlife.

Marrs also notes that Gardner made the important point that the matters of mysterious powders, breads, and substances that had a bearing upon life, the extension of life, and which were linked to the Gods millennia ago, are only now slowly becoming known to us.

Gardner, himself, said of the ancients that they "knew that both the physical body and the light body [that which we would term the spirit or the soul] had to be fed to increase hormonal production and the ultimate food for the latter was called shem-an-na by the Babylonians, mfkzt by the Egyptians and manna by the Israelites" (Gardner, 2016).

CHAPTER 6

The Immortals in India

It's now time to turn our attention to the mysterious world of ancient India and yet another enigma-filled cocktail. It, too, has a direct tie to the domain of life that never ends through the Indian gods who, in all likelihood, were powerful extraterrestrials. As we'll see, they may very well have been the Anunnaki, albeit under a different name. Welcome to the world of what is known as Amrita. The name of this curious drink is highly appropriate, because it translates into English as nothing less than "immortality." Also referred to as Amrit and Soma, Amrita is a mysterious liquid that, Hindu texts assure us, gave immortality to the Devas and the Devis who are male and female gods that play significant roles for those who adhere to Hindu teachings and history.

Just like Amrita, the word "Deva" has notable meaning and relevance to the story this book tells. Deva, essentially, means "divine" and "heavenly." It is supernatural and from a world above, one might be justified in saying. According to Hindu scriptures and texts, such is the incredible, rejuvenating power of Amrita that the tiniest amount swallowed is all but guaranteed to bring the aging process to a sudden halt and even to an *irreversible* halt. But how did the story of this incredible and life-changing substance begin? To answer that question, we have to go back to the very earliest times of Hindu culture.

Devas vs. Asuras

As is the case in practically all ancient and major religions, Hinduism is filled with fantastic tales of both benevolent supernatural entities and those that are downright evil and malevolent. Such accounts proliferate within the Vedas, ancient texts penned in Sanskrit. The former entities were the Devas and the Devis, whereas those to be avoided at just about all costs were the Asuras. And, as is also the case in so many ancient religions, the two opposing sides had a deep hatred of each other, to the point of each wishing the other side exterminated. Hindu history and lore tells of how, in the immediate aftermath of the creation of the Earth, the Asuras—who are clearly the Hindu equivalent of the demons of the Christian Bible—are intent on holding sway over the planet. The Devas, who not only hated the Asuras, but who were terrified of them too, decided to take action and find a way to extinguish them forever.

The *Times of India* says: "Both devas and asuras are children of Kashyapa [a legendary rishi, or poet, in English], born of different wives. Devas are called adityas, because their mother is Aditi. Asuras are daityas and danavas because they are children of Diti and Danu. The devas and asuras are constantly fighting each other." The *Times of India* also reveals that the Devas achieved states of immortality as a result of their ingestion of Amrita or, as the legends also suggest, a mysterious nectar that may well be the very same substance that the pharaohs of Egypt had a deep awareness of and which saved the Israelites from starvation (Pattanaik, 2016).

There are other parallels too: in Christian teachings there are various supernatural realms of existence, such as Earth, Heaven, Hell, and Purgatory. It's far from dissimilar in Hinduism: Patala, a terrifying underworld, is the closest thing to Hell; Swarga (or, alternately, Svarga) is a definitively heavenly realm; and, of course, there's our world.

There are, however, more than a few differences, as Quora makes abundantly clear: "The Hindu cosmos or Brahmanda is visualized as a skyscraper. In the center stands Bhu-lok, earth. Above are realms of increasing happiness . . . Below are realms of decreasing happiness, the lowermost floor being Patal-lok . . . This realm is full of gold and gems, hence the city of Asuras is called Hiranyapura, city of gold" ("Which land of modern world is the Patal-Lok the place under the sea, as it was mentioned in Old Hindu manuscripts and stories?" 2013).

One has to wonder if the reference to a city made out of gold, in the context of an immortal life, is a nod in the direction of White Powder Gold.

Although the Devas were described as gods, unlike in Christian teachings, within Hinduism there are *levels* of gods, rather than just one, overall creator. Among those gods who were determined to destroy the Asuras were the gods of fire, of the wind, and of the sky: Agni, Vayu, and Indra, respectively. Above them, however, were Brahma, Vishnu, and Shiva. Their titles: Creator, Preserver, and Destroyer. If the Devas were to defeat the Asuras, they would have to achieve something that, in those early times, they still had yet to attain: everlasting lives. The mighty trio of Brahma, Vishnu, and Shiva—who *were* immortal—shared with Indra, Agni, and Vayu something amazing: the incredible secrets of Amrita.

Immortality in India

Rather notably, Amrita, and all that it offered and promised, were hidden in the absolute lowest levels of the world's oceans. This, it will be recalled, is eerily similar to—if not even practically identical to—the story told in the *Epic of Gilgamesh*. Namely, that the king who so desperately sought immortality, Gilgamesh himself, was forced to plunge deep below the waves to secure a mysterious immortality-giving plant that could only be found on the seabed. Such was very much the case, too, in the Hindu epics. All of which brings us to what was known as the Samudra Manthan, meaning the Churning of the Ocean.

What happened next in the Hindu accounts sounds not unlike a scene playing out in some 1950s-era Godzilla movie: Vishnu transformed into a giant turtle, atop of which stood a mountain that, as the monster-turtle swam into the depths of the seas, churned the water in a violent and turbulent fashion. Echoing the Godzilla parallels, a huge, snake-like beast, Vasuki—the king of a terrible underworld known as Nagloka, and the overlord of snake-entities known as the Naga—aided in the process of causing near-cataclysms on the high seas. We should also not forget that in the *Epic of Gilgamesh*, the king fails to achieve immortality due to the presence of a mighty serpent that steals the mysterious, life-giving plant. Clearly, one story is based upon the other. Or, in widely varying locations on the planet, not just the Gods, but certain elite people too, knew where to find the answers to immortality: under the water.

The evil Asuras were deeply cunning entities and realized that they, too, could massively benefit from ingesting Amrita. And, knowing that incredible manpower (or god-power) was needed to raise the Amrita, the Devas initiated an uneasy truce. It quickly played out, to the extent that the Asuras and the Devas worked together, to further churn the massive waves, and to ensure that the huge turbulence finally brought the much sought after Amrita to the surface. This, we are told, is exactly what happened. The Devas, however, had no real intention of ever providing the Asuras with even a miniscule amount of Amrita. Instead, the demon-like Asuras were given what was *assumed* by them to be Amrita, but which, in reality, was nothing of the sort.

The Sanatan Society reveals how that plot played out. According to legend, both sides—the demonic ones and the angelic ones—"immediately tried to seize [the Amrita] but the demons were first. While they were quarreling over who should drink it first, Vishnu assumed the form of Mohini, a beautiful woman, and through sleight of hand, she gave the demons varuni, or liquor, while the gods got the amrit" (Marchand, 2016).

The Sanatan Society states that the crafty demonic entities soon realized they had been fooled and on a big scale, too. Hardly surprising, they were quick to fight back and managed to get their claws on the much sought after Amrit. It was during this violent game of tug of war that a small amount of Amrit was spilled and cascaded across the landscape, and created priceless gem mines in the process. Amid all of the chaos, however, the demons caught on to the deception and grabbed the Amrit kumbh, or the pot of elixir. Jayant, the son of the god of the skies, Indra, grabbed the pot of Amrit under the noses of the deities—both angelic and demonic—and fled the scene. Indra is said to have deposited the Amrit in four, specific locations after himself imbibing from the container. They were locations that became sacred to the people of India and have become central to the Kumbh Mela, a faith-based pilgrimage of Hindu persuasion.

"This Center Provides the Mystery of Eternal Youth"

Matt Caron notes something intriguing about this life-extending substance—namely, that it appears to be something born out of reality, rather than from the worlds of folklore, mythology, and legend. Caron says: "The precious immortality-giving nectar is said to flow from the pituitary gland into the back of the throat during *very* deep states of meditation. In order to help the release of amrita from the pituitary gland, a mudra known as Kechari (tongue lock) is practiced" (Caron, 2016).

This all brings us to the work of one Wendy Munro, who observes that the pituitary gland is, in essence, a "psychic intuitive center." She adds: "This center allows you to know when other people are thinking about you. It also enables the gift of prophecy and remembrance of past lives. Visions can be experienced with dreams of precognition" (Munro, 1999).

Not without a high degree of significance, Munro also states that *"this center provides the mystery of eternal youth* [italics mine]" (ibid.).

"What Is This Nectar?"

An ancient Buddhist scripture, the *Milinda Panha*, or Questions of Milinda, which was written roughly a century before 1 AD reveals significant and thought-provoking data on the nature of Amrita. The story that the *Milinda Panha* tells is, essentially, revealed in the form of a conversation between two notable figures: King Menander I (also known as Milinda) who reigned in northern India from 155 to 130 BC, and a wise man named Nagasena, who was born in Kashmir. At one point, the king asks Nagasena: "Revered Nagasena, what is the nectar shop of the Buddha, the Blessed One?" (*The Questions of King Milinda*, 2015). He replies:

> "Nectar, sire, has been pointed out by the Blessed One. With this nectar the Blessed One sprinkles the world with the devas; when the devas and the humans have been sprinkled with this nectar, they are set free from birth, aging, disease, death, sorrow, lamentation, pain, grief and despair. What is this nectar? It is mindfulness occupied with the body. And this too, sire, was said by Milinda, the Blessed One: 'Monks, they partake of nectar (the deathless) who partake of mindfulness that is occupied with the body.' This, sire, is called the Blessed One's nectar shop" (ibid.).

Although Zecharia Sitchin is primarily known for his research into the world and history of the Anunnaki, his studies did take him in the direction of ancient India, as he noted, and which is hardly surprising. He said: "Notwithstanding the many connecting threads the ancient Greeks had found between their theogony and that of Egypt, it was much further away—in India—that nineteenth-century European scholars have found even more amazing parallels" (Sitchin, 2007).

Sitchin continued:

No sooner had Sanskrit, the language of ancient India, been mastered at the end of the eighteenth century than Europe began to be enchanted by translations of hitherto unknown writings . . . Central to this literature were the Vedas, sacred scriptures believed by Hindu tradition to be "not of human origin," having been composed by the gods themselves in a previous age.

In time, the various components of the Vedas and the auxiliary literature that stemmed from them (the Mantras, Brahmanas, Aranyakas, Upanishads) were augmented by the non-Vedic Puranas ("Ancient Writings"). Together with the great epic tales of the Mahabharata and Ramayana, they make up the sources of the Aryan and Hindu tales of Heaven and Earth, gods and heroes (ibid.).

It's worth noting that the *Mahabharata* and the *Ramayana*, to which Sitchin referred, tell of mighty battles fought not just on the land but in the skies of India, too. In terms of the latter, we're talking about Vimanas—mysterious flying machines capable of incredible aerial feats and which, with hindsight, sound not unlike *Top Gun*–style aircraft of our very own civilization. Add to that the claims made by numerous students of the ancient extraterrestrial scenario that the Vimanas were armed with atomic missiles that flattened landscapes, destroyed cities, and killed millions, and what we have is a situation very close to the scenario involving the Anunnaki and the destruction wrought by them as they waged war on each other in ancient times.

On this very matter, an early student of ancient alien scenarios, W. Raymond Drake said:

> This wonderful epic of the "Ramayana" the inspiration of the world's great classic literature, intrigues us most today by its frequent allusions to aerial vehicles and annihilating bombs, which we consider to be inventions of our own 20th century impossible in the far past. Students of Sanskrit literature soon revise their preconceived ideas and find that the heroes of Ancient India were apparently equipped with aircraft and missiles more sophisticated than those we boast today (Drake, 1973).

Then there is the following from David Hatcher Childress, an authority on Vimanas and their place in India's history: "According to ancient Indian texts, the people had flying machines which were called 'vimanas.' The ancient Indian epic describes a vimana as a double-deck, circular aircraft with portholes and a dome, much as we would imagine a flying saucer" (Childress, 2003).

"Super Humanoids"

In Sitchin's version of events, the Anunnaki had achieved immortality—or just about the closest thing to it. The Devas of India did likewise. Both the Devas and the Anunnaki are perceived by UFO researchers as extraterrestrials. In both India and those areas of the planet where the Anunnaki dominated, we see evidence and accounts that are eerily suggestive of ancient atomic warfare, as I note in my 2016 book, *Weapons of the Gods*, and as W. Raymond Drake suggested decades ago. This begs an obvious and glaring question: taking into consideration all of the above, were the Anunnaki and the Devas of India actually one and the same? Just maybe, that's exactly what they were. Such a scenario makes a great deal of sense, as AboveTopSecret.com demonstrates: "Comparing texts from the Ayurveda scriptures with the translations of Zecharia Sitchin, we can see a very strong similarity between the Sumerian gods and the Hindu gods . . . the ancient Hindus weren't talking about mythic creatures or fantasy deities, but real beings, super humanoids coming from stars and their interaction with mankind" ("Were the Anunnaki alien race, the same Hindu gods???", 2010).

Devas, gods, Anunnaki: they might all have been one and the very same.

CHAPTER 7

Ambrosia of the Gods

We may never know for sure what the mysterious Manna, Amrita, and White Powder Gold really were; however, what we can say with absolute certainty is that numerous similar age-reversing or age-*stopping* cocktails crop up throughout recorded history and across the planet. And almost each and every one of them is associated with all-powerful, seemingly supernatural deities. Take, for example, the legendary ambrosia of the gods of ancient Greece. It's a mystery-shrouded substance that makes its first surfacing in the story of Zeus, the Greek god of the skies and thunder. He ruled the gods from his domain on the Mytikas Peak of Mount Olympus, the highest of all the Greek mountains. As for the gods, they were known, quite understandably, as the Olympians. As well as Zeus, they were comprised of Apollo, Hermes, Poseidon, Hera, Ares,

Demeter, Athena, Hephaestus, Dionysus, Artemis, and Aphrodite. But who, exactly, were they?

So far as can be determined, the Olympians had their origins in the era of the Titans. In Greek mythology, there were three kinds of deities. The first were known as the Primordial ones. The third were the Olympians. Sandwiched in between were the Titans. It was thanks to Rhea and Cronus—both of them Titans—that the Olympians came into existence. The pair had more than a few children. They were Zeus, Poseidon, Hera, Hades, Demeter, and Hestia.

We're told: "Hades was supposed to live on Mount Olympus and had every honor and right to but was given the realm of death under his control, when the three brothers had to split the cosmos after the victory over Titans. And Hestia lived there just for a short period" ("The Olympian Gods," 2016).

Given that there was a great deal of competition for a place on Mount Olympus, Hestia elected to give up her place and, as a result, the aforementioned Zeus, Apollo, Hermes, Poseidon, Hera, Ares, Demeter, Athena, Hephaestus, Dionysus, Artemis, and Aphrodite became acknowledged as the definitive Olympians.

Now, let's take a closer look at the mysterious ambrosia.

Loggia.com says: "While scholars are not entirely certain what the ancient Greeks thought the composition of ambrosia (or its liquid counterpart, for that matter) actually was, it is believed that these mythical items had some connection to a sweet treat enjoyed by mortals throughout the ages—honey" ("Ambrosia—Food of the Greek Gods," 2016).

It's a fact that, for the ancient Greeks, honey was a much-loved food item. But there was far more to it than just that. A study of Greek mythology shows that ambrosia had the ability to provide immortality to those who partook of it. Indeed, Aphrodite, the goddess of love, is said to have bathed in ambrosia to ensure a youthful state when engaging in seduction.

The "Spacemen" of Ancient Greece

In 1976, W. Raymond Drake, who penned a number of books on alleged alien visitations to the Earth in ancient times, said:

> The most fascinating stories of Spacemen shine not in our chill Science-Fiction but in those war, colorful, passionate tales told long ago in Ancient Greece, inspiring the classical poets of Antiquity to delightful romance. Awed by the beauty and perfection of wondrous Creation, the Greeks described the universe as "Kosmos" meaning "Ornament," revealing their reverence for the sublime splendor of Heaven and Earth, which the Gods made for them (Drake, 2011).

More than 20 years later, the issue of Drake's "Spacemen" and ancient Greece was still being discussed. In 2000, Erich von Daniken—probably the most famous figure in the field of ancient astronauts—penned a book titled *Odyssey of the Gods*. In its pages von Daniken theorized that the gods of ancient Greece were extraterrestrials who set foot on our world thousands of years ago. Citing archaeological data and the writings of the ancient Greeks, including the legendary philosopher Aristotle, von Daniken presented a theory suggesting the so-called gods of Greece interbred with humans, "performed genetic experiments, and bred 'mythical' creatures, such as centaurs and Cyclops." von Daniken went on to suggest that the oracular site of Delphi was an aircraft refueling station, that Jason's famous and legendary pursuit of the golden fleece was, in reality, a quest to seek out an "essential aircraft component," and that the city of Troy was destroyed "in a war between aliens or their descendants" (von Daniken, 2000).

Ambrosia, Amalthea, and the Atlas Mountains

Greek mythology is filled with stories of superhero-like gods. It's also filled with accounts of gods with never-ending lives, and which have clear and undeniable extraterrestrial overtones attached to them. For example, Greek legend tells of how there was a specific period before ambrosia was known to the gods of Greece. That did not stop them from living forever, however. In the pre-ambrosia era, the gods were said to inhale the souls—or the life-force, or essence—of their slain foes through their nostrils, something that would provide life everlasting.

This issue of the immortal soul and its connections to the nostrils also extends to the domain of not just the Greek gods, but elsewhere, too. In 1890, Sir James George Frazer said:

> The soul is commonly supposed to escape by the natural open-ings of the body, especially the mouth and nostrils. Hence in Celebes [an Indonesian island east of Borneo, now called Sulawesi] they sometimes fasten fish-hooks to a sick man's nose, navel, and feet, so that if his soul should try to escape it may be hooked and held fast. A Turik on the Baram River, in Borneo, refused to part with some hook-like stones, because they, as it were, hooked his soul to his body, and so prevented the spiritual portion of him from becoming detached from the material. When a Sea Dyak sorcerer or medicine-man is initiated, his fingers are supposed to be furnished with fish-hooks, with which he will thereafter clutch the human soul in the act of flying away, and restore it to the body of the suf-ferer. But hooks, it is plain, may be used to catch the souls of enemies as well as of friends (Frazer, 1890).

Such stories should not, needless to say, be interpreted literally. As we shall see later, however, there are deep and, at times, acutely disturbing accounts of how the human soul plays a role in the story of extraterrestrial immortality, and even of how elements of the U.S. Government may possesses extensive knowledge of such controversial and astounding issues, some of which spill over into the domain of what are termed alien abductions.

The Greek gods were distinctly different to mere mortals: aside from being immortal, their bodies lacked blood. Instead, they had coursing through their veins something called Ichor. It was *a gold-colored liquid* that was fatally poisonous to humans, but which was dominated by the rejuvenating aspects of ambrosia. It's worth pondering on the possibility that the tales of this gold-colored liquid had their roots in distorted tales of White Powder Gold.

As for ambrosia, according to one of several legends, we have nothing less than a goat to thank for its existence. The goat was named Amalthea; she faithfully looked after Zeus just as would any mother. Zeus was lucky to have survived birth: his father, Cronus—the leader of those divine entities known as the Titans—learned from the deities Uranus and Gaia that he, Cronus, was destined to be overthrown by a son. And, so, he gruesomely devoured all of his male offspring the moment they were born, something which hardly made him an ideal father. Zeus, fortunately, survived. His mother, a Titan named Rhea, was able to smuggle Zeus to Mount Ida—the Mountain of the Goddess—where he was brought up by the aforementioned Amalthea the goat. In other versions of the story, Zeus was raised by Gaia herself, or by a nymph named Adamanthea—nymphs being nature spirits that never aged and, for the most part, were able to avoid death. Rather notably, ambrosia was said to be particularly abundant in a near-magical garden guarded and nurtured by a group of ageless nymphs known as the Hesperides. They resided on the Atlas Mountains, a 1,600-mile-long range in northwest Africa.

The Intriguing Eagle

According to the tale, Zeus would feed upon ambrosia and nectar, which ensured death never came for him. The latter—the food of the gods—was provided by a flock of white doves, whereas the former came from what was intriguingly described as a huge eagle. It was an eagle that possessed a pair of gleaming wings, and which travelled the skies at incredible speeds. From our perspective, the "eagle," which would reportedly land on Mount Olympus to deliver the much-needed ambrosia, sounds far more like a highly advanced aircraft of some type or even a spacecraft than it does a huge bird.

Also, Zeus and the eagle go together, hand in glove: "The Aetos Deus was a giant, golden eagle which served as Zeus' personal messenger and animal companion. According to some it was once a mortal king named Periphas, whose virtuous rule was so celebrated that he was came to be honored like a god" (Aetos Deus, 2016).

Achilles' Heel and the World of Ambrosia

Ambrosia did not just provide immortality to those who partook of it. It was also said to have the amazing ability to rejuvenate the skin, to repair scarred and damaged tissue, and to ensure that the body always remained disease- and illness-free. It even surfaced in the well-known tale of the death of Achilles, a character who played a major role in the Trojan War of 1260 to 1180 BC. His mother, Thetis, was a legendary nymph of the sea, whereas his father, Peleus, ruled over the

Achilles, Ambrosia, and immortality (Franz Matsch, 1892, Wikimedia Commons).

Myrmidons; they were mighty soldiers whose exploits are chronicled in Homer's classic poem, the *Iliad*.

Thetis, as a near-immortal nymph herself, recognized the deep importance of ensuring that Achilles, too, had life everlasting. It was her daily routine to take a large jug of ambrosia and pour it over her newborn, beloved baby. The ambrosia would be absorbed through the skin, thus providing Achilles with immortality or, rather, *almost* providing him with immortality. Thetis made what turned out to be not just a big mistake, but a fatal and irreversible mistake. During the regular process of bathing her son in ambrosia, Thetis would pour the magical liquid over him with one hand, while holding him in her other hand by one of his ankles. The result was that this same ankle was never exposed to ambrosia. Thetis' grip ensured that this one, solitary part of Achilles' body remained forever ambrosia-free. In the Trojan War, this proved to be deadly for Achilles. Paris, the son of the King and Queen of Troy, Priam and Hecuba, reportedly shot a poison-loaded arrow into Achilles' ankle—his single weak spot, and one which inevitably guaranteed his death, hence the often-used term, "Achilles' Heel."

Yet again, we see evidence of enduring, powerful gods in possession of strange elixirs that ensured them life evermore or almost so, when it came to Achilles. As is the case with so many ancient legends and myths, taking such stories surrounding ambrosia and Zeus as the gospel truth stretches credibility to the absolute max. That there may be some significant truths behind the tales, however, is far from being out of the question. In fact, quite the opposite is almost certainly the case.

A Youthful Fountain

It should be noted that the controversy surrounding ambrosia sounds not unlike the tales and legends that revolve around the so-called

Fountain of Youth, accounts of which span several thousands of years. One of the most famous such stories concerns the Macrobian people of Aethiopia, in the Sahara Desert. It's perhaps not without significance that although the story is set in Aethopia, the source of the story was a 5th-century historian named Herodotus, who hailed from none other than Greece.

From various "Ichthyophagi," an ancient word for those people who lived in coastal regions, Herodotus was able to state that, the king of the Macrobians and his people "lived to be a hundred and twenty years old, while some even went beyond that age—they ate boiled flesh, and had for their drink nothing but milk" (Rawlinson, 1875).

From an 1875 edition of *History of Herodotus*, edited by Sir Henry Creswicke Rawlinson and John Gardner Wilkinson, we have this:

> When the Ichthyophagi showed wonder at the number of the years, [the king] led them to a fountain, wherein when they had washed, they found their flesh all glossy and sleek, as if

Welcome to the Fountain of Youth (Lucas Cranach, 1546, Wikimedia Commons).

they had bathed in oil—and a scent came from the spring like that of violets. The water was so weak, they said, that nothing would float in it, neither wood, nor any lighter substance, but all went to the bottom. If the account of this fountain be true, it would be their constant use of the water from it which makes them so long-lived (ibid.).

This sounds almost identical to the ultimately tragic story of Achilles who, as a baby, was bathed in ambrosia as a means to stave off the aging process.

Mysteries of the East and Those Who Don't Die

Now, it's time to turn our attentions to China, where deities, gods, or aliens all held significant sway over the populace. They included Shangdi, otherwise known as the Highest Deity, Pangu the Creator, and the Jade Emperor. Consider the following, regarding the aforementioned emperor and immortality: "The Jade Emperor is the supreme ruler of Heavens, the hades and the protector of mankind according to Chinese folklore religion and the highest ranking deity of the Taoist pantheon. From the ninth century onwards, he was the patron deity of the Chinese imperial family" ("Taoist Deities/Gods," 2006).

We're also told that, upon the passing of his father, the Jade Emperor took his rightful place on the throne and created a culture and civilization that thrived on tranquility. Most important of all, he attained a state of immortality.

From Alchemy to Immortality

That the gods of China had achieved—or were created with—states of immortality inevitably led the Chinese people to also try and secure ways to live forever. Daniel Appel says of this very issue: "Chinese alchemists spent centuries formulating elixirs of life. They were frequently commissioned by the Emperor, and experimented with things like toxic mercury, gold, sulfur and plants. The formula for gunpowder, sulfur, saltpeter and carbon was originally an attempted elixir of immortality" (Appel, 2014).

He continues that old Chinese manuscripts reference what is known as the Mushroom of Immortality, "a key ingredient in the elixir of life" (ibid.).

Those same attempts to achieve immortality may not have reached their goal, but what was it that set the ancient Chinese on quests for immortality in the first place? It's notable and almost certainly not a coincidence that the Chinese people of millennia ago were particularly fixated upon the idea of drinking certain concoctions that they knew their gods embraced when it came to living forever. They were (a) cinnabar, which is a poisonous mercury sulfide mineral; (b) jade; and (c) our old friend, gold. One cannot ignore the fact that the references to gold and immortality clearly parallels the saga of the Anunnaki and White Powder Gold, and even the story of Moses and the Israelites' golden, false god. Yet again, we see tales, myths, and folklore from widely varying cultures and countries all relative to immortality on the part of the gods/extraterrestrials, and man's desperate attempts to follow in their pathways and crack the code to endless life.

The Chinese quest for immortality was not without a fair amount of irony, however: "To the philosophers of China, nothing was more valuable than life. Therefore, Chinese alchemists searched tirelessly for a potion that would grant immortality or an elixir of life. Many alchemists died after consuming the often deadly potions that they created" ("Ancient Chinese Alchemists and their Search for Immortality," 2016).

As we'll see later, there is good evidence that, deep within the heart of government, someone is secretly still doing likewise. And they're just about as desperate to find the answers as were those long gone souls from thousands of years ago.

CHAPTER 8

Everlasting Life in Ancient Egypt

We'll now take a look at the connections between such issues as Manna, longevity, incredible feats in medicine, the world of the Anunnaki, and the reversal of death in the culture of ancient Egypt. Within the Egyptian *Book of the Dead*, a somewhat enigmatic phrase repeatedly appears. It amounts to three simple words: "What is it?" Egyptian papyruses state: "I am purified of all imperfections. What is it? I ascend like the golden hawk of Horus. What is it? I pass by the immortals without dying. What is it? I come before my father in Heaven. What is it" ("ORMUS: The Elixir of Life," 2016).

The answer is that "What is it?" was nothing less than Manna. What this demonstrates is that, as with the Israelites, the Egyptians were very familiar with this life-saving, and perhaps even immortality-giving, substance that was known throughout the ancient world and which left its mark in the Old Testament and in early Egyptian texts.

It is worth noting, too, the following, which comes from the Library of Halexandria and which has noted a linkage between Egyptian Manna and White Powder Gold, the latter playing a vital role in the matter of immortality and the Anunnaki: "The White Powder of Gold is a multitude of things . . . In science, the white powder of gold is the ORME—i.e. gold (or any of the Precious Metals) in a monoatomic form—which can result in Superconductivity within an organic body" (Ward, 2003).

As we'll now see, the Egyptians had an undeniable obsession with life, death, the afterlife, and keeping death just about as far away as possible.

The Egyptians and the Soul

Brad Steiger says:

> As early religions began to teach that there was a spirit within each person who died that might someday wish to return to its earthly abode, it became increasingly important that efforts be made to preserve the body. Burial ceremonies, which had at first been intended solely as a means of disposing of the dead, came to be a method of preserving the physical body as a home for the spirit when it returned for a time of rebirth or judgment (Steiger, 2010).

There is perhaps no better example of this than in the world and beliefs of ancient Egypt. As a result of its regular, high temperatures and dry atmosphere, Egypt was an ideal place for the embalming of corpses to take place. Those deigned for mummification were the powerful, the royal, and the elite. The process was intricate: both the intestines and the brain were carefully extracted from the body. The empty skull, and what was once the stomach, were filled with fragrant spices, after which the open cavities were sewn back together and placed in salt for slightly more than two months. Then, the process of mummification—encasing the body in cloth, in other words—took place and the body was placed into a specially crafted case.

Just about every conceivable item that one might need in the afterlife was placed in the direct vicinity of the mummified soul. That included food, spears and swords (to ward off thieves that might wish to plunder the sacred area), and cups and plates to allow the dead to partake of food and drink.

As for the soul of the dead, in Egypt—as is also the case in a number of ancient religions—it had two aspects attached to it. There was the Ba, which was just about the closest thing to the soul of Christian teachings. Interestingly, when the elite of Egypt finally went to meet their maker, very careful attention was given to ensuring that all the mouth, both eyes, the nose, and both ears were open and free of any obstructions. This would permit the Ba to return to the body it once inhabited. And then there was the Ka, which Brad Steiger describes as "a kind of ghostly double that was given to each individual at the moment of birth. When the person died, the Ka began a separate existence, still resembling the body that it formerly occupied, and still requiring food for sustenance" (Steiger, 2010). There was also the Sakkem—a life-force—and the Khu, which represented intelligence.

That the Egyptians spent an inordinate amount of time ensuring that their kings, queens, and revered and powerful figures remained, physically speaking, well-preserved has led to theories that they were paying homage to—and even doing their utmost to try and emulate—their gods who never aged and never changed. This is not unlike the Anunnaki, whose physical appearances remained static for a minimum of hundreds of thousands of years. As we'll soon see, there are more than a few pointers suggesting direct links between the Anunnaki and the people of Egypt.

In Vitro Fertilization in Ancient Egypt?

Zecharia Sitchin observed that both the Egyptian *Book of the Dead* and the Pyramid Texts—the latter discovered carved onto the walls of the Saqqara-based Pyramids around 2,400 BC—"related how the dead Pharaoh, embalmed and mummified, was prepared to exit his tomb (deemed only a temporary rest place) through a false door on the east and begin a Journey to the Afterlife. It was presumed to be a journey simulating the journey of the resurrected Osiris to his heavenly throne in the Eternal Abode" (Sitchin, 1998).

Osiris, to whom Sitchin referred, was not just the Egyptian god of the afterlife, but also the god of *regeneration*, which is a most intriguing title for this legendary deity. It's a title that strongly suggests the Egyptians had some awareness (and, perhaps, even a great deal of awareness) that death could be avoided and that the secrets of immortality rested in the regenerative hands of the all-powerful gods; or, perhaps, to be accurate, in the regenerative technology of an ancient extraterrestrial race from a planet called Nibiru.

Sitchin noted that Osiris' resurrection was "coupled with another miraculous feat," namely, the birth of Horus, who was the son of Osiris. Sitchin also observed that Isis, the wife of the dead Pharaoh, received significant assistance from a deity named Thoth. This assistance specifically related to the process of "putting the dismembered Osiris together, and then instructed [Isis] how to extract the 'essence' of Osiris from his dismembered and dead body, and then impregnating herself artificially. Doing that, she managed to become pregnant and give birth to a son, Horus" (ibid.).

This process, as described by Sitchin and derived from the millennia-old Egyptian texts, sounds astonishingly like what, today, we term in vitro fertilization. The Mayo Clinic says of the IVF process: "In vitro fertilization (IVF) is a complex series of procedures used to treat fertility or genetic problems and assist with the conception of a child.

During IVF, mature eggs are collected (retrieved) from your ovaries and fertilized by sperm in a lab" ("In vitro fertilization [IVF]," 2016).

Horus the "Avenger"

It transpires that Isis had deliberately withheld knowledge of the birth and existence of Horus from a famous figure in Egyptian lore named Set. He was an Egyptian deity of storms and of the desert. Set was also someone who lusted after his sister Isis and who attempted to have sex with her, with the specific intent of ensuring she fathered a child that would be destined to be Set's heir. Fortunately, Isis was able to escape the clutches of Set and made her stealthy way to a swamp-filled region where she had previously hidden young Horus. There was, however, tragedy on the horizon: upon arriving at the place where she had carefully hidden Horus, Isis was overcome by grief to discover that he had succumbed to the fatal sting of a deadly scorpion. But, just perhaps, there was a way to do the incredible: namely, bring Horus back from the domain of the dead. This was nothing less than outright resurrection. The grieving, devastated mother implored Thoth to help her son. According to the ancient texts, that is exactly what happened:

> Then Isis sent forth a cry to heaven and addressed her appeal to the Boat of Millions of Years and Thoth came down; He was provided with magical powers, and possessed the great power which made the word turn into deed. And he said to Isis: I have come this day in the Boat of the Celestial Disk from the place where it was yesterday. When the night cometh, this light shall drive away [the poison] for the healing of Horus. I have come from the skies to save the child for his mother (Sitchin, 1998).

Returned to life and, incredibly, as good as new, Horus went on to become the Avenger, a term which was most apt, because Horus—upon reaching manhood—engaged the aforementioned Set in violent, near-endless battles. Matters finally culminated in a head-to-head confrontation in which Set and his soldiers were captured by Horus and brought before Ra, the Egyptian god of the Sun, who, presumably, would decide their fates. Ra, however, turning the tables to a significant degree, said that the decision should be left to Isis and Horus alone. Despite all the death and fighting that had gone on, Isis simply could not bring herself to order the death of Set, something that enraged Horus to the extent that he is said to have taken a sharp sword to his mother and violently decapitated her with one mighty swing. Notably, according to the ancient legends, Thoth quickly intervened and managed to reattach Isis' head and returned her to life—a procedure that Thoth had apparently previously, and equally successfully, performed on a goose!

Such a story sounds as fantastic as it does unlikely. It should be noted, however, that most legends have at least *some* basis in reality. And it's a fact that our technology and medicine is now proceeding down a very similar path to that which allowed Thoth to perform an amazing miracle-like act on Isis.

Heading into the Future

In 2016, in a sensational article titled "Doctor Ready to Perform First Human Head Transplant," *Newsweek* reported that "Italian neurosurgeon Sergio Canavero is set to perform a two-part human head transplant procedure." *Newsweek* continued: "Three years ago, Canavero, now 51 . . . announced he'd be able to do a human head transplant in a two-part procedure he dubs HEAVEN (head anastomosis venture) and Gemini (the subsequent spinal cord fusion)" (Urken, 2016).

One of those who came forward to potentially undergo such a groundbreaking procedure was Valery Spiridonov. A Russian man, Spiridonov had a very good reason for wanting to come on board: he has Werdnig-Hoffman disease, which causes the muscles of the body to waste away. In other words, though Spiridonov's head remains as it was, his body will, with time, degrade more and more. So, in that sense, he would make an ideal candidate: the transfer of a healthy head from a failing body onto a brand new, healthy body.

The UK's *Guardian* newspaper chimed in on the publicity afforded Canavero, saying: "Head transplants have been attempted before—on Russian puppies in the 1950s, on an American monkey in the 1970s, on hundreds of Chinese mice between 2013 and 2014. The puppies lived less than a week, the monkey just over that. The mice tended to linger about a day." As the *Guardian* also stated, when it came to the matter of the surgeries undertaken on the dogs, the mice, and the monkey, the primary goal was not so much to ensure that the animals survived (either in the short or long term), but to demonstrate that such a procedure was at the very least feasible—which was most unfortunate for the animals chosen for the experiments (Lamont, 2015).

Time may tell if Canavero succeeds in achieving something very similar to that which Thoth very possibly performed on Isis thousands of years ago in the heart of Egypt.

Thoth and Quetzalcoatl: One and the Same?

If Thoth was indeed able to successfully reattach the heads of both a woman and a goose, the question has to be asked: who, exactly, was Thoth? Was he a supernatural deity with the ability to achieve the seemingly impossible by nothing more than the wave of his hand? Or, perhaps, was Thoth a highly skilled scientist—one born on another world hundreds of thousands of years earlier—who had the ability to reverse death and perform incredible medical feats? Zecharia Sitchin strongly suspected that the latter was the case. He claimed to have identified Thoth as none other than one Ningishzidda who, in Sumerian teachings, just happened to be the son of Enki, no less than one of the most powerful figures in the history of the Anunnaki. According to

Sitchin, Thoth/Ningishzidda "was the keeper of Divine Secrets of the exact sciences, not the least of which were the secrets of genetics and biomedicine that had served well his father Enki at the time of the Creation of Man" (Sitchin, 1998).

This, no doubt, served the Anunnaki well when it came to the issue of immortality.

Controversial suggestions were also made by Sitchin to the effect that Thoth/Ningishzidda was also none other than Quetzalcoatl. According to chiefly Mesoamerican mythology, Quetzalcoatl was an incredibly advanced being, one possessed of what the people of that era would surely interpret as divine talents. These divine talents, however, were likely to have been science and technology that would surely boggle the minds of 21st-century humankind, never mind the people of centuries and millennia ago. Aztec history tells of how Quetzalcoatl did his utmost to try and bring civilization, technology, order, and a new world to the Mesoamericans, and who first impacted on the people of the area at some point between 100 BC and 100 AD. His name translates as feathered serpent; hence the name of a notable structure that can be found at Teotihuacan, just a short drive from Mexico City, and which was built around 100 BC: the Temple of the Feathered Serpent. Admittedly, there is some degree of controversy about the precise date upon which Quetzalcoatl first surfaced and for one, specific reason: long before Quetzalcoatl was on the scene, and as far back as 900 BC, Mesoamericans were worshipping *other* serpentine deities, and particularly so in Tabasco, Mexico.

Alessandro Demontis says of this thought-provoking controversy, when it comes to the matter of both Ningishzidda and Quetzalcoatl, that there are "mythological common traits, like the attribution to both deities of a central role in the process of creating and instructing humanity. Ningishzidda was a pacific god, depicted with two entwined snakes, and when it was depicted in human form he had two horned snakes rising from his shoulders" (Demontis, 2009).

Notably, and again echoing the connections between numerous famous characters and deities in times past, Sitchin said that on the matter of Quetzalcoatl and the "entwined snakes"/Ningishzidda issue, "there was undoubtedly a connection between all that and the fashioning by Moses of a copper serpent in order to stop a pestilence that felled countless Israelites during the Exodus" (Sitchin, 1998).

As we've also seen, it was during the Exodus that the Anunnaki may have saved an untold number of Israelites by providing them with near-endless amounts of Manna. So, where does all of that leave us? Well, it leaves us with an ancient people, the Egyptians, who believed in human immortality—albeit largely in spirit, ethereal form—and who were determined to ensure that by mummifying and preserving their dead, they would remain in a state of never aging, just like their gods that they so revered and feared. That Zecharia Sitchin suggested a connection between the Anunnaki and the gods of Egypt—to the extent that they were perceived by him as being nothing less than one and the same—offers yet further evidence that it was the immortality factor of the Anunnaki and their extensive lives that led the Egyptians to focus so intently on trying to emulate the gods and achieve some form of unending existence.

CHAPTER 9

Ireland's Immortal "God"

In the controversial story of ancient extraterrestrials and everlasting life, one of the most fascinating tales concerns a legendary and powerful Irish ruler. His name was Manannan mac Lir. He was a notable figure in a mysterious race of supernatural entities known as the Tuatha De Danann. He held sway over the land at the height of the Bronze Age, which, in Europe, extended from 3,200 to 600 BC. For the people of that particular era, mac Lir was a powerful, even possibly magical, deity. From what we know about aliens and immortality, however, a solid case can be made that mac Lir was a being of unearthly proportions.

We're told that there are parallels between Manannan mac Lir and the legendary Scandinavian deity, Odin: both were formidable figures, utterly ruthless on the battlefield. They can travel from our reality to the domain of the gods and back again. And they both have wives and multiple lovers. "On a more fantastic level, both have horses that can travel over land and sea, and a boar or pigs that *renew themselves* [italics mine] after being eaten" ("Manannan mac Lir [and some Norse Connections" 2015]).

In early Irish history and folklore, there were gods that ruled over the land, over the skies above, and over a dark underworld, the latter being not unlike the Christian Hell. Then there were the gods of the oceans. And leading the pack of those gods that held sway over the waters was Manannan mac Lir, the son of yet another legendary sea-god, Ler. Notably, "mac Lir" translates into English as "son of the sea." He was both revered and feared by the early people of Ireland, as most gods usually tend to be, regardless of their geographical location.

Mary Jones, an authority on this intriguing character of old, says that nobody, so far, "has successfully come up with an etymology for the name 'Manannán' but only that it means 'Him from the Isle of Man.' Either the god is named for the Isle of Man, or vice versa. However, his surname of 'mac Lir' indicates that he is the Son of the Sea" (Jones, 2003).

Manannan mac Lir is a strange and almost magical entity. He oversees a magical realm that is known as the Plain of Apples which, with hindsight, sounds not at all unlike the biblical Garden of Eden. On top of that, he possesses a spear—Crann Buide, to give it its specific title—that has supernatural attributes, such as being able to fly through the sky and slay mac Lir's foes in an instant. He also owns a strange bag that never gets full and which sounds very much like Dr. Who's time-traveling Tardis in the popular BBC series, in which the doctor's time-machine is bigger on the inside than it is on the outside.

High-Technology on the High Seas

Although mac Lir is primarily tied to Irish lore and legend, it is widely accepted by historians that the Isle of Man—an island located in the Irish Sea and just a short trip by boat from the coastline of the United

Kingdom—was named in mac Lir's honor. For the 80,000-plus people that live on the Isle of Man today, the tales of mac Lir are still told, embraced, and even believed.

The primary reason why mac Lir was so deeply tied to the seas is very simple, yet also very intriguing. He spent most of his time traveling the waters of our world in what was clearly an extremely advanced craft, the Scuabtuinne. In English we would call it the Wave-Sweeper. Given the time-frame, one might well assume that the Wave-Sweeper was something akin to an ancient wooden galleon of centuries past. This is not so. In fact, precisely the opposite is the case. Consider the following: the Wave-Sweeper lacked any and all kinds of masts and sails. It required no crew to row it. No wind was needed to move the huge craft across the waters. And it had the ability to not just operate on the surface of the water, but also to descend to incredible depths. Crashing waves and turbulent thunder-and-lightning-filled storms had no effect whatsoever upon the mighty Wave-Sweeper. The deep parallels between the Wave-Sweeper and a high-tech submarine of the 21st century are as clear as they are glaringly obvious.

Welcome to the World of the Forever Young

When he wasn't negotiating the harsh, deep waters that surround Ireland, mac Lir dwelled in the heart of what was termed the Land of Youth, a most apt term to be sure. And although primarily linked to the seas, mac Lir also played a role in ferrying the souls of the recently dead to the domain of the underworld and subsequent life-everlasting, which are yet further pointers in the direction of alien immortality. This is made all the more notable by the fact that his wife, Fand, was a queen of the fairies. Why is that so notable? Let us take a look at what we know.

First and foremost, it's important to note that the image we have of fairies today, namely of small, enchanting figures with shining wings, is very far removed from the fairies of yesteryear, who were much more sinister and even dangerous in nature, and not at all Tinkerbell-like in appearance or character.

One of the staple parts of the stories pertaining to Irish fairies—and, indeed, to fairies and the wee folk just about here, there, and everywhere—is that, unlike us, they stayed perpetually young. Throughout their lives, and in terms of their physical appearances, they never aged and they had incredibly long life spans. They did, however, have a problem. And it was no minor problem. In so many legends and tales of the Irish fairies, they were described as being blighted by one thing more than any other: reproductive issues. Despite their near-immortal lives, female fairies very often gave birth to stillborn babies. Many died in the days and weeks that followed birth, demonstrating that immortality was not *always* guaranteed for these ethereal, strange creatures. And sterility was often a problem, too.

As a result, the fairies resorted to using us, the human race, to overcome their many problems of the reproductive variety. The little people of Ireland would stealthily invade homes in the dead of night and steal human babies from under the noses of their sleeping, unaware parents. The reason was to take them to the fairy kingdom, where they would be brought up by the fairy folk. If the fairies couldn't have their own children, they were determined to have ours instead. On a similar path, the men of Ireland were routinely enchanted and kidnapped by fairy queens and their minions—usually after sunset, on isolated, dark roads or in the heart of dense woods—and taken to the domain of these legendary, dwarfish elementals. The captured men were required to have sex with the fairy queens as a specific means to try and inject new blood into the fairy world, thereby hopefully ensuring the fairy race continued.

Fairies or Aliens? Or, Are They One and the Same?

Anyone and everyone with an interest in the UFO phenomenon will note the clear and undeniable parallels between the tales of the diminutive wee folk—who kidnapped people, invaded homes in the middle of the night, and created half-human/half-fairy offspring—and modern-day accounts of so-called alien abduction. The attendant accounts of ET/human hybrid-babies, genetic experimentation, and the extraction of eggs, sperm, and DNA from the abductees add further weight to the comparisons. That Manannan mac Lir was married to one of the elite fairy queens adds yet another immortality-linked issue to the life of this mysterious and powerful figure.

On this very same path, Laura Knight-Jadczyk says: "The similarities between fairy abductions and UFO abductions is also interesting to note. People who claimed interactions with fairies generally reported marks on their bodies consistent with reports of alien abductions. Fairy abductions and UFO abductions also exhibit striking similarities to activities of incubi and succubi" (Knight-Jadczyk, 2016).

Knight-Jadczyk has also identified other parallels, too, such as the abductee very often being given a strange concoction to drink—something that has a long history attached to it. She also notes that the little people of centuries ago moved around in ethereal balls of light, which are clearly the ancient equivalent of today's UFOs. Knight-Jadczyk also highlights the fact that this strange interaction between the human race and entities that eerily resemble each other—despite being separate by centuries or even by millennia—often revolves around sexual encounters and the manipulation of the targeted person, something which has led to insanity and disaster for those who the fairies and the aliens kidnap and manipulate.

Manannan mac Lir's Amazing Tools of Warfare

Manannan mac Lir was also someone who had an arsenal of incredible, futuristic weaponry at his disposal. That arsenal included a sword known as Fragarach. It was far from any normal sword, however. Also referred to as The Retaliator, the sword, if that's what it really was of course, had the ability to pierce not just the body of a man, but also metal, brickwork, and timber. Fire violently flashed forth from its tip, almost immediately ensuring that anyone caught in its path suffered an agonizing, burning death. Not unreasonably, parallels have been made between the Fragarach and modern-day laser- and death-ray-style technology.

Manannan mac Lir also commanded a supernatural horse, Enbarr of the Flowing Mane, who was owned by yet another Irish god, Lug. The animal had the ability to not only pull a great, gleaming chariot on land, but also across the oceans. The closest thing we have to Enbarr today is a hovercraft, which can travel across both land and water with extreme ease. We should not, then, rule out the possibility that this is exactly what Enbarr was—the horse angle being a distortion born out of elaboration, myth, cultural conditioning, and story-telling.

Then there is the mysterious féth fíada. It can best be described as a kind of supernatural fog, or a cloak, as it was also described. In short, it held the power and the secrets of invisibility. Anyone shrouded by the fog/cloak would be rendered invisible to the human eye. If you think that invisibility and cloaking, similar to that perfected and utilized by mac Lir, are merely the stuff of wild science-fiction, it's time to think again.

In October 2006, the following was noted in the U.S. media: "Flip a switch and make something disappear? It's been the stuff of science fiction for decades. Now, two Duke University scientists and their colleagues have built the world's first device to render an object invisible" (Markey, 2006).

So far, at least, the technology is only invisible to microwaves; however, the team behind the research at Duke University believes that, in time, it will be able to beat detection by the likes of sonar, radar, motion-detection cameras, and more. The secret: metamaterials, which promise the ability to cloak, and perhaps in precisely the same way that mac

Lir was able to operate without being seen. In other words, what we are now finally beginning to understand and grasp, in terms of invisibility, may have been second-nature to Manannan mac Lir.

Age Defying and a Mysterious "Cauldron"

Certainly, the most fascinating part of this story is that which concerns mac Lir's ability to ensure he never aged. It was all due to what became known as his Cauldron of Regeneration. In some versions of the story, the cauldron had the ability to literally regenerate that which, today, we would refer to as human cells and DNA. Providing a person made regular and careful use of the cauldron, they could remain young and, in theory, forever so. According to another version, the cauldron "could bring the dead back to life, although they could not speak of the experience . . . It has also been written that the cauldron could be destroyed if a living being was placed inside it, rather than the bodies of the dead" ("Cauldron-born," 2016).

It's illuminating to note that a near-identical, mysterious cauldron turns up in yet another Irish saga. This one tells of an imposing, approximately 11-foot-tall goddess known as Cymidei Cymeinfoll. As was precisely the case with mac Lir, this particular deity was able to utterly dismiss aging by immersing herself in her very own cauldron, thus ensuring nothing less than immortality. Her particular cauldron had another trick up its sleeve too, so to speak. It could reanimate the dead and was most often utilized to resurrect warriors killed on the battlefield. This is, perhaps, something akin to today's defibrillation-style technology which, essentially, "kick-starts" the heart back to life via a powerful electric current.

Sabrina of Goddessaday.com says of the imposing Cymidei Cymeinfoll that she was a Welsh deity of battle who dwelled deep below an old Irish lake, along with her partner, Llasar Llaesgyfnewid. That is, at least, until an attempt was made to murder the pair by the then-ruler of Ireland, one Matholwch. Both husband and wife were fortunate enough to escape the deadly clutches of Matholwch and "escaped to Wales, taking with them the Cauldron of Regeneration which they guarded. When a warrior was killed in battle, he was thrown into the cauldron, and would emerge alive but without the ability to speak. They gave the cauldron to Bendigeidfran, King of Wales, also known as Bran" (Sabrina, Goddessaday.com, 2008).

Goddessaday.com has important data on this specific issue, too: "When Bran's sister Branwen was to be married to Matholwch, their half-brother Efnisien threw a fit and mutilated several of Matholwch's horses. In appeasement, Bran gave Matholwch the cauldron as a peace offering to take back to Ireland" (ibid).

Sadly, the union was not destined to be long or loving. When Bran learned that his sister was being physically abused by Matholwch, he and his half-brother launched an all-out assault on Matholwch, the intent being to free Branwen from his evil clutches. According to the story, however, things did not go at all well for Bran and Efnisien, chiefly because the Cauldron of Regeneration continually brought the slain, Irish soldiers back to life. Eventually, however, the tide turned, although not in wholly positive fashion. Efnisien was able to disable the mysterious cauldron, something which ensured the Irish warriors were no longer able to reanimate from the dead. There was, however, a terrible cost: the only way Efnisien could destroy the cauldron was by jumping headlong into it, something which brought the machine to a shuddering halt and took Efnisien's life in the process.

The End for mac Lir?

A final word on Manannan mac Lir: although advanced alien technology ensured him everlasting life, that did not mean he could not die, which, as we have seen, was also the case with the Anunnaki. There is, of course, a paradox here: how can someone who is immortal die? The answer is very simple and also parallels the story of the Anunnaki: regeneration, and putting an end to the process of growing old, did indeed permit the gods, as well as their half-human offspring, to live for centuries and millennia. However, those same elite figures—such as Manannan mac Lir—had to be very careful they did not fall victim to everyday hazards that could end anyone's life, including those of the immortals. We're talking about being stabbed to death, burned alive, or decapitated. Not even the gods themselves could prevent irreversible death in such situations.

As for mac Lir, after a near-endless life, he finally met his match at the Battle of Magh Cuilenn. He was fatally wounded by the sword of one Uillenn Faebarderg and was said to have been buried, standing upright, deep in an Irish peat-bog. The Grim Reaper wasted no time in calling on mac Lir. He had after all been waiting, deeply impatiently, for so many millennia. Or did mac Lir actually live on? In 1904, one Lady Gregory, in *Gods and Fighting Men*, said that despite the tales of mac Lir being killed, "he had many places of living, and he was often heard of in Ireland after" (Lady Gregory, 1905).

Just perhaps, Manannan mac Lir really did beat the Grim Reaper. Maybe, he still does, but under a new guise and identity. It's these issues of new identities and guises that we will now focus on to a greater, more in-depth, degree.

CHAPTER 10

The Man Who Never Dies

It's now time to turn our attentions to the strange and undeniably controversial story of a man who is alleged to have not only achieved immortality, but whose story encompasses the legendary land of Atlantis, extraterrestrial entities, and the secret domain of alchemy. Very appropriately, and just like the enigmatic character himself, the story definitively endures. His name is the Count of St. Germain.

Precisely who, exactly, the Count really was is a matter of deep debate among those who have studied the extraordinary life of this very mysterious man. That he existed, however, is not a matter of any doubt. So far as can be determined, it was in the very early years of the 18th century—around 1705 to 1715—that the Count of St. Germain first surfaced publicly, quickly inserting himself into the world of the rich and the powerful of Europe. He did so with amazing ease, too. Those who met the Count at the time suggested that he appeared to be in his late 30s or, at the very most, in his early 40s. The Count seemingly preferred to keep his real age and true origins to himself, something which ensured that an air mystery and intrigue quickly surrounded him. And, as history has shown, it never left him.

Rumors soon began to circulate to the effect that the Count of St. Germain was possibly of an elite, royal bloodline and maybe, even, the ostracized son of a powerful and ancient European family. The Count carefully chose to remain enigmatically tight-lipped on such claims. High-society figures flocked to him, women were immediately entranced by him, men envied him, and he soon became the subject of deep interest. That he appeared to have endless amounts of money, which permitted him to travel the globe, seems undeniable. He was clearly very well read, had an expensive and lavish wardrobe, and told of his adventures in Persia (today, Iran), where he learned the secrets of alchemy, the ancient ability to transmute base metals such as tin into nothing less than priceless gold. Further rumors swirled around, all pointing in one direction: namely, that the Count's exposure to the mysterious domain of alchemy had allowed him to tap into the world of immortality.

Although such a scenario is certainly controversial, from the early 1700s to the latter part of the century, the Count of St. Germain did appear to maintain his youthful state, while all of those around him aged, withered, and finally died. Indeed, throughout the 1740s, the Count traveled widely throughout Scotland, England, and France. Reportedly, those who met the Count three decades earlier maintained that by the mid-1700s he had not changed. Age-defying or ageless, the Count by now had taken on legendary status. And his ability to stay young, vigorous, well-connected, and rich continued.

An extensive trip to India in 1755 took up much of the Count's time, as did a growing friendship with the French king of the day, Louis XV. Officially, the Count died on February 27, 1784—still appearing no different to how he looked in 1705. Students of his life, however, have suggested that his death was simply a convenient and ingenious way for him to adopt a new identity—something which, perhaps, he routinely did to ensure that no one ever learned of his secrets and his immortal life, unless of course he specifically chose to share his story with others. As we'll soon see, this may very well have happened and maybe on more than a few occasions, too.

A Man of Many Identities

On this particular matter of the Count constantly changing his identity, Maxamillien de Lafayette says: "He was supposed to have been, in previous lives, St. Alban, an English saint of the third or fourth century AD; Proclus, a Neoplatonic philosopher who lived during the 5th century AD; Roger Bacon, a thirteenth century English philosopher; and Sir Francis Bacon, a philosopher, author, and statesman who lived in the sixteenth century" (de Lafayette, 2010).

de Lafayette continues: "Some go as far as associating him with ancient civilizations, such as Atlantis, and Biblical personalities, such as the Prophet Samuel. The Theosophists accepted him as one of their Ascended Masters" (ibid.).

On the matter of Sir Francis Bacon and the Count, there's this: "According to Elizabeth Clare Prophet, St. Germain ascended on May 1st 1684. Although Sir Francis Bacon is said to have died in 1626, Prophet claims that the body in the coffin at Sir Francis Bacon's funeral was not his own and that he attended his own funeral" ("Count St. Germain—Alchemist," 2016).

A Mysterious Life-Giving and Age-Defying Liquid

There was something else, too; something which suggests the count may not have been entirely human and perhaps not even human *at all*—aside, that is, from his physical appearance. One of the strangest of all claims was that the count rarely ate food; preferring instead to almost exclusively live on a mysterious drink, allegedly some kind of tea, as doubtful as that most assuredly sounds. Could it, perhaps, have been something akin to a nectar of the gods, one which promised and provided constant rejuvenation of the body, its cells, and DNA? Was it White Powder Gold or Amrita, perhaps?

These questions bring us to the work of David Pratt. He says that in 1762, during the reign of Tsar Peter III—and when Russian troops set out to invade Denmark—Prince Carl of Hesse-Cassel, whose grandfather was England's King George II, was "given command under Field-Marshal le Comte (Claude-Louis) de Saint-Germain, and rode with him in Pomerania" (Pratt, 2012).

Prince Carl, himself, all those centuries ago had some notable and eye-opening things to say about the Count of St. Germain:

> He was perhaps one of the greatest philosophers that ever existed. A friend of humanity; only desiring money to give it to the poor; also a friend of animals; his heart was never occupied except with the good of others. He thought he was making the world happy in providing it with new enjoyments, the most beautiful fabrics, more beautiful colors, much cheaper than previously. For his superb dyes cost almost nothing. I have never seen a man with a clearer intelligence than his, together with an erudition (especially in ancient history) such as I have seldom found (Tingley, 1914).

And then we have this from the prince, which makes specific reference to the mysterious "tea" which appeared to keep the count endlessly young:

> He knew thoroughly all about herbs and plants and had discovered medicines which he continually used and which prolonged his life and his health. I still possess some of his recipes, but the physicians strongly denounced his science after his

[assumed] death. There was a physician there named Lossau, who had been an apothecary, and to whom I gave twelve hundred crowns a year to work with the medicines which the Count of Saint-Germain gave him, among others; and principally with his tea, which the rich bought and the poor received gratis. This doctor cured a number of people, of whom none, to my knowledge, died. But after the death of this physician, disgusted with the proposals I received from all sides, I withdrew all the recipes, and I did not replace Lossau (ibid.).

A Cult and the Count

There can be absolutely no doubt that the most inflammatory and controversy-filled aspect of the saga of St. Germain revolves around certain events that allegedly occurred on the slopes of California's massive Mount Shasta in the early part of the 20th century. It was in 1930, so the story goes, that on the mountain—which stands in excess of 14,000 feet, and is part of the huge and sprawling Cascades range— the elusive, everlasting count mysteriously surfaced. It's a story that came from a man for whom controversy was nothing out of the ordinary: Guy W. Ballard. Before we get to the Ballard–St. Germain connection, however, it's important to first have an understanding of who precisely Ballard was.

In the early 1930s, Ballard created a movement known as I AM. One might be far more accurate in terming it as a full-blown cult. And, as is the case with most cults, it was overseen by a dominating and manipulative leader/guru: Ballard himself, of course. As is also the case with cult leaders, Ballard was charismatic to the point where I AM, at its peak, boasted of having no fewer than *12 million followers*, worldwide. One of those who has studied the strange world and life of Ballard is John Gordon Melton. Of this curious character, who wrote under the alias of Godfre Ray King, Melton provides the following:

"Ballard compiled his experiences in a book, *Unveiled Mysteries*, published in 1934, and he afterward claimed to receive regular messages, termed 'discourses,' from St. Germain and other Masters. Because one of the Masters from whom Ballard received dictations was Jesus, members of the I AM movement consider themselves Christian" (Melton, 2016).

Although I AM gained momentum in 1932, and Ballard's *Unveiled Mysteries* book was published two years later, it's to 1930 that we really need to turn our attention. That's the year in which, reportedly, Ballard met a man who could not die: the everlasting, identity-changing Count of St. Germain.

A Meeting on a Magical Mountain

It's important to note that Ballard's alleged encounter with the Count may not have been the random, innocent event that many have suggested it was. Certainly, Ballard, even before he ever encountered the Count, knew that there was something deeply mysterious and spiritual about Mount Shasta. Ballard admitted as much himself: he said, for example—under his Godfre Ray King pseudonym—that his book was penned in the "embrace" of the huge mountain, the apex of which he described as being forever "robed" by the majestic, towering peak, which was "pure, glistening white, the symbol of the 'Light of Eternity'" (King, 2011).

According to Ballard, at the time in question, he had been dispatched to a small town near Mount Shasta on what he rather enigmatically described as government business. It was while in the vicinity of the imposing, snow-covered mountain that Ballard—who was already a devotee of all things occult-based and of a mind, body, and spirit nature—chose to use his spare time to chase down certain, intriguing rumors. They were rumors suggesting that a certain elite and secret order of ascended masters had quietly made their home deep within the heart of the mountain—as in literally within its claimed myriad tunnels, deep passages, and cavernous realms.

Ballard quickly developed an affinity for Mount Shasta and its attendant enigmas, and which never left him: "I fell in love with Shasta and each morning, almost involuntarily, saluted the Spirit of the Mountain and the members of the Order . . . Long hikes on the trail had become my habit, whenever I wanted to think things out alone or make decisions of serious import. Here, on this Great Giant of Nature, I found recreation, inspiration, and peace that soothed my soul and invigorated mind and body" (ibid.).

Rather notably, Ballard added that such was the appearance and magical nature of Mount Shasta, he could almost accept he was on an entirely different world. It's somewhat appropriate, with those words cited, that now is the time for the Count of St. Germain to make an appearance.

The day began in an appropriately spiritual fashion, as Ballard recalled:

> The morning in question, I started out at daybreak deciding to follow where fancy led, and in a vague sort of way, asked God to direct my path . . . as the day advanced, it grew very warm and I stopped frequently to rest and to enjoy to the full the remarkable stretch of country around the McCloud River, valley, and town. It came time for lunch, and I sought a mountain spring for clear, cold water. Cup in hand, I bent down to fill it, when an electrical current passed through my body from head to foot (ibid.).

The immortal Count had duly arrived.

Quite out of the blue, Ballard experienced a certain feeling that we all get from time to time: namely, that of being watched and watched very intently. While taking a break on the banks of the McCloud River, Ballard, developing a sudden sense that he was not alone, spun around. Sure enough, there was a mysterious figure standing mere feet away from Ballard. The man looked like any normal individual, but that didn't stop Ballard from thinking that he was anything *but* normal. Ballard was not wrong.

The count then did something that is a staple but a very curious part of many alien encounters, as we have already seen: he offered Ballard something delicious and mind-altering to drink. In the Count's alleged own words: "My Brother, if you will hand me your cup, I will give you a much more refreshing drink than spring water" (ibid.).

Ballard said of this strange offering that he obeyed the Count's words and drank the creamy cocktail, which had a profound effect on Ballard's mind, even to the point of placing him into a somewhat altered state of consciousness. Rather notably, one gets the sense that this mysterious, rejuvenating liquid may very well have been somewhat akin the mysterious Manna of the Bible, White Powder Gold, and Indian Amrita. Certainly, the Count's very own words suggest this was very likely the case:

> That which you drank comes directly from the Universal Supply, pure and vivifying as Life itself. It is, in fact, Life-Omnipresent Life—for it exists everywhere about us. It is subject to our conscious control and direction, willingly obedient, when we Love enough, because all the Universe obeys the behest of Love. Whatsoever I desire manifests itself, when I command in Love. I held out the cup, and that which I desired for you appeared. See, I have but to hold out my hand, *and, if I wish to use gold—gold is here* [italics mine]. (ibid.)

Once again, we see the presence of, and a reference to, gold. And the gold angle doesn't end there. The Count then proceeded to demonstrate his apparent incredible skills of the alchemical kind by manifesting in the palm of his hand a small disc made of gold. St. Germain continued that he knew Ballard was on a deep quest to understand what was termed the Great Law, even though he, Ballard, may not have been fully aware of just how deeply enmeshed in that same quest he really was. It was this lack of full awareness, the Count explained, that prevented Ballard from obtaining all he could from what was termed "the Omnipresent Universal Supply" (ibid.).

Ballard was also told that his trek on the mountain, which had led him directly to the Count, was no accident or random event. It was a meeting of minds, one that was chiefly dictated by what was described by the Count as Ballard's very own inner God. In other words, although he did not consciously realize it, it was Ballard himself who had initiated the encounter. At that point, the mysterious figure who stood before Ballard instructed him to remain completely still for a while, after which he promised to reveal his true identity.

Transformation on Mount Shasta

In approximately 60 seconds or so, said Ballard, the seemingly regular man who stood before him morphed into something else: namely, what Ballard described as the Master. Practically in a state of near-religious ecstasy, Ballard stared in awe at the man who, Ballard offered, had a deity-like appearance. Dressed in a flowing outfit covered in jewels, the Count's eyes were now shining brightly. In moments, the encounter was over. St. Germain was not gone for long, however. Just a couple of days later, there was a second meeting of minds.

The late UFO contactee George Hunt Williamson inherited a great deal of Ballard's personal correspondence, much of which made its way to him from contacts in the I AM cult and that, to an edited degree, made its way into the pages of *Unveiled Mysteries*. One such letter, of March 1931 to a man named Stanley Carter, reveals what Ballard claimed happened just two days after the initial encounter with the Count, yet again on the slopes of Mount Shasta.

A Potentially Deadly Encounter

In Ballard's own words, contained in a letter found in Williamson's files, he says: "As I contemplated the wonderful privilege and blessing that had come to me, I heard a twig crack and looked around expecting to see him. Imagine my surprise when, not fifty feet away, I saw a panther slowing approaching. My hair must have stood on end. I wanted to run, to scream—anything—so frantic was the feeling of fear within me. It would have been useless to move, for one spring from the panther would have been fatal to me" (Ballard, 1931).

Ballard continued to Carter that his mind was in a state of absolute terror, and his body was rooted to the spot. Then, something very strange happened; something that just may have saved Ballard's life. He suddenly felt overwhelmed by a powerful force, one which oozed both love and light and both of which, Ballard suspected and ultimately concluded, also enveloped the mind of the potentially lethal panther. On this very matter, Carter was told:

> The stealthy tread [of the panther] ceased and I moved slowly toward it, feeling that God's Love filled us both. The vicious glare in the eyes softened, the animal straightened up, and came slowly to me, rubbing its shoulder against my leg. I reached down and stroked the soft head. It looked into my eyes for a moment and then lay down and rolled over like a playful kitten The fur was a beautiful dark, reddish brown; the body long, supple and of great strength. I continued to play with it and when I suddenly looked up Saint Germain stood beside me (ibid.).

The story got stranger—in fact, it got a great deal stranger—when the saint claimed that the presence of the panther was no coincidence. It was, said the allegedly immortal entity, "a test," one designed to determine Ballard's personal, inner strength when faced with mortal danger, and to ensure that Ballard could conquer his "outer self." The test, however, was not exactly that of the Count himself, as Ballard explained to Carter. St. Germain supposedly said:

I did not have anything to do with the panther being there. It was part of the inner operation of the Great Law, as you will see before the association with your new-found friend ceases. Now that you have passed the test of courage, it is possible for me to give much greater assistance. Each day you will become stronger, happier, and express much greater freedom (ibid.).

Food of the Gods

It was at this point that the Count presented Ballard with something that, yet again, eerily echoed the Manna of the Bible. It was, the letter to Carter revealed, nothing less than "four little cakes of a beautiful golden brown, each about two inches square." Notably, when Ballard ate the cakes something profound suddenly occurred; something which further emphasizes the potential rejuvenating nature of the mysterious substance from which the cakes were made: "Immediately, I felt a quickening, tingling sensation through my entire body—*a new sense of health* [italics mine] and clearness of mind. Saint Germain seated himself beside me and my instructions began" (ibid.).

Those same instructions became the ideology of the I AM group. Things were not destined to last, however. When Guy Ballard died in 1939, his wife, Edna, took over the reins of the I AM movement and claimed that she, too, had been in contact with the legendary Count of St. Germain. As was the case with her late husband, Edna claimed to have received profound, philosophical messages from this alleged ascended master. Edna lived on until 1971, still standing by her claims to the end. In the wake of her passing, the I AM movement's directors ran the organization. It should be noted that not a single message from the count—or, indeed, from any other masters—has been received since the death of Edna Ballard. Skeptics suggest this is because the Ballards fabricated everything. On the other hand, supporters of the I AM movement suggest it was the fact that, after Edna died, no one else was put in place to receive such messages that has led to the overwhelming silence.

With that all said, it's now time to take a closer look at the matter of that Manna-like substance, and rejuvenating liquid, that the Count urged Ballard to eat and imbibe.

Extraterrestrial Elixirs and Space-Borne Sustenance

There can be no doubt that the one person, more than any other, who has delved deep into the world of extraterrestrials and their undeniable penchant for offering people curious cocktails of unknown liquids, as well as strange items of food, is Joshua Cutchin, the author of a book titled *A Trojan Feast*. Through the years and decades, a great deal of undeniable nonsense has been written about the connections between aliens and food, such as the absurd notion that the so-called alien Greys have a particular taste for endless amounts of strawberry ice-cream. At least, one *assumes* it's absurd! Nevertheless, and despite the high-strangeness that surrounds matters relative to aliens, immortal entities, and food, the subject has a long history attached to it.

Cutchin notes that offerings from "the others" almost always come in several, clearly delineated kinds: food (almost always bland), liquid (very often of a bitter-tasting nature), and pills. Sometimes, it's a combination of all three. The "food," however, may not be exactly what it appears to be. And it's not just a case of "the aliens" feeding us because they are feeling generous or think we need to pack on a bit more muscle. It's nothing quite that simple. The act (and "act" may be a very appropriate word to use) of presenting us with food appears to help and dictate how the encounter both commences and, more often than not, concludes (Cutchin, 2015).

Jacques Vallee's *Passport to Magonia* book did a fine job of noting the parallels between today's alien encounters and centuries-old interaction with the fairies, the wee folk of times long gone who, rather notably, never aged. Cutchin's work, however, has taken things to a whole new level, as he notes the incredible similarities that exist between food offerings then and now, and provided to us by entities that many might assume have no connection, but which so obviously do.

The usually bland nature of the food provided by today's extraterrestrials has its parallels in the food of the fairies, which was made to appear and taste enriching and delicious, but in reality was nothing of the sort: it was all a ruse. As for why such theatrical games are played, this gets to the very heart of the puzzle. Cutchin suggests that food offerings become a part of the experience because the phenomenon—which is so strange and alien and to the point of being almost beyond comprehension—"prefers symbolism and mythology as the currency of conversation" (ibid.). This is a very important statement that is absolutely central to the overall story.

As Cutchin dug further, he uncovered a rich vein of data that has previously been missed or dismissed, including the notable fact that such food offerings correspond very closely—in terms of specific food items—to a Sattvic diet. It is a diet that is particularly popular in Eastern traditions, and particularly so among Hindus. It's interesting to note that a Sattvic diet is also associated with the awakening and the refining of clairvoyant skills—something that may allow for greater interaction with the others. In other words, following a Sattvic diet may lower the barriers between here and there, wherever there may actually be.

Sleep paralysis has come into play in Cutchin's quest for the truth, too. He notes that an imbalance of electrolytes in the human body may provoke night-time terrors, as they are known. Such terrors usually occur between 1:00 a.m. and 3:00 a.m. and render the victim into a briefly paralyzed state, while a menacing and threatening entity hovers over or in close proximity to the bed. As Cutchin also notes, one of the most common such electrolytes in our diet is sodium. The less salt, then, the less the body is likely to be plunged into a fear-filled state of paralysis. He asks: "Could the folklore of salt repelling faeries be grounded in a much more pragmatic solution for avoiding sleep paralysis?" (ibid.).

Cutchin also speculates, but in a logical and well-reasoned fashion, on how these things might really dine: possibly on the *foyson*, or the energy of food. The possibility that absorption through the skin plays a significant role in the ingestion and digestion of food by seemingly magical entities has also been addressed by Cutchin, who also suggests that the theater of entity food is designed to ease the shock of encountering the unknown. That's to say, we are shown something to which we can relate, something that comforts us, and something that calms us: food. The nourishment from beyond, then, is "a symbolic vehicle to facilitate interaction" (ibid.).

So-called entity foods, Cutchin suggests, may be nothing less than entheogens—hallucinogenic substances that provoke profound, vision-like experiences in rituals of a shamanic variety. This all leads seamlessly into matters relative to DMT, ayahuasca, and how what many might assume are simply vivid hallucinations are actually glimpses of other realities. Quite possibly, they are realities in which our many and varied visitors of the non-human type originate. Such foods may also provoke changes in consciousness, purely as a result of the power of suggestion—very much like the placebo effect.

Of course, that does not mean *all* alien food items are offered in charade form, although, admittedly, the story of Guy Ballard and Count St. Germain does have an undeniable, stage-managed quality to it. It seems likely that from the ancient days of Manna from Heaven, White Powder Gold, and Amrita to the 1930s, and the presence of an immortal entity on Mount Shasta, our extraterrestrial visitors have a deep—but presently not fully understood by us—connection to how the nourishment of the human body can rejuvenate, revive, and even conquer death.

It's now time to turn our attentions to what is arguably an even bigger controversy: it all revolves around a 1950s-era contactee and a never-changing extraterrestrial who goes by the name of Valiant Thor.

CHAPTER 11

An Immortal in the Pentagon

On November 21, 2008, UFO researcher-author Greg Bishop wrote: "The Reverend Frank Stranges, author of such contactee classics as *Stranger at the Pentagon* and *Flying Saucerama*, has returned to his permanent home with the space brothers, according to an e-mail today from Tim 'Mr. UFO' Beckley. Stranges founded the National Investigations Committee on Unidentified Flying Objects (NICUFO) in 1967" (Bishop, 2008).

Stranges' organization was very much inspired by the much bigger and far more visible NICAP, the National Investigations Committee on Aerial Phenomena, which was created in 1956. The NICAP focused, for the most part, on studying reports involving sightings of UFOs in the skies above, analyzing photographs, and collecting flying saucer-themed data from military personnel and the public. Stranges, however, had a far more controversial claim to fame.

He maintained that, from 1959 onward, he had extensive contact with an extremely human-looking extraterrestrial named Valiant Thor—a strange and mysterious figure who, reportedly, had met with several U.S. presidents and numerous high-ranking military personnel. The result: Thor had the ability to effortlessly move throughout the inner circle of the Pentagon. That, in Stranges' story, Valiant Thor both sounds and looks like actor Michael Rennie's alien character, Klaatu in the classic 1950 sci-fi movie, *The Day the Earth Stood Still*, has led skeptics to believe that Stranges made up the whole, controversial saga. As we shall soon see, however, that may not have been the case. And, as we shall also see, there is a direct link between the story of Valiant Thor and extraterrestrial immortality.

"Only a Few Men in Washington Knew of His Existence"

In relation to that alleged meeting with Thor in the Pentagon in 1959, Stranges, himself, offered the following:

> Being a minister of the Gospel of Jesus Christ, as well as a student of the Bible for many years, coupled with my experience as an special investigator, I felt as though my senses were functioning properly and that I knew exactly what I was about to do. I was on my guard for fakes and frauds. In walked a man, about six feet tall, perhaps 185 pounds, brown wavy hair, brown eyes.
>
> His complexion appeared normal and slightly tanned. As I approached him and he looked at me it was as though he looked straight through me. With a warm smile and extending his hand, he greeted me by name. His genuineness astonished me, but quickly I understood. As I gripped his hand, I was somewhat surprised to feel the soft texture of his skin, like that of a baby but with the strength of a man that silently testified to his power and intensity (Stranges, 1991).

An extraterrestrial in the Pentagon (U.S. Government, 1998, Wikimedia Commons).

As for why precisely Thor had made it his business to visit the Earth, Stranges informed his followers:

> He told me that his purpose in coming was to help mankind return to the Lord. He spoke in positive terms ... always with a smile on his face. He said that man was further away from *God* than ever before, but there was still a good chance if man looks in the right place. He told me he had been here nearly three years and would depart in just a few months (Stranges, 1991).

Claiming that he would not use force to speak with men in authority in America, he was happy to consult with them at their invitation. He further stated that thus far only a few men in Washington knew of his existence in the Pentagon (Stranges, 1968).

And few leaders had availed themselves of his advice during these past three years. He felt there was still so much to do and yet his time of departure was getting near. He told me that *Jesus Christ* would not force men to be saved from their mistakes, even though He had already made a way for mankind to be redeemed through His shed blood.

When I asked him where he was from, he replied, "I am from the Planet that is called Venus."

I asked him how many visitors from Venus were presently on Earth and he said, "There are presently seventy seven of us walking among you in the United States. We are constantly coming and going" (ibid.).

What, precisely, does this all have to do with the matter of immortality? Let's see.

The Long-Lived Thor

There's no doubt that the story of Valiant Thor and Frank Stranges peaked in the 1960s in terms of both popularity and visibility. Undeniably, for the vast majority of figures within the field of Ufology, the issues of contactees, Space Brothers, and human-looking aliens are perceived as being very much historical in nature, rather than contemporary. That vast majority, however, are wrong. The intriguing fact is that reports of the kinds of entities encountered by the likes of George Van Tassel and George Hunt Williamson—and Frank Stranges, of course—decades ago still surface on a regular basis. The problem is that Ufology as a unified entity so often prefers to dismiss such undeniably sensational cases, perceiving them as an embarrassment to the subject. This is unfortunate, and particularly so when one takes into consideration the sheer number of reports that exist. But there's more to come. Of those continuing reports of encounters with the Space Brothers, more than a few describe modern-day encounters with Valiant Thor who, according to the witnesses, appears not to have physically changed or aged since his heyday when Frank Stranges was busy promoting his story. It's very much the Count of St. Germain saga all over again.

This is an issue that ItsAStrangeWorld.com has picked up on: "Thor had been working with the government since 1937. His physical traits included six fingers, an oversized heart, one huge lung, copper oxide blood like that of an octopus, and possessed an incredibly high IQ measuring around 1200, *and a lifespan of approximately 490 years* [italics mine]" (Strange World, 2014).

A Star-Man in a Starbucks

One of those who claims contact with the long-lived Thor is a Californian woman who I will call Sandy Mason. Now in her late 30s, Mason has had a profound connection to the UFO phenomenon since she was a child. Until her early 30s, Mason's encounters were very much of the alien abduction variety. We're talking about missing time, and eggs, DNA, and genetic material extracted from her body under frightening and distressing circumstances—and always in the dead of night. That all changed, however, when Mason reached the age of 34. The abductions came to a sudden end and were immediately replaced by something else or, rather, by some*one* else.

According to Mason, in February 2012, she had a very strange experience while living in California's Simi Valley, which is located in Ventura County. It was a warm, pleasant morning and Mason was hanging out in one of the several Starbucks that can be found in the valley. As she sat, reading and sipping her coffee, a man came up to her, quite out of the blue, and asked if she knew who he was.

A somewhat understandably wary Mason definitely did *not* know who the well-dressed, dark-haired man was. She soon found out, however. The man sat down, took a sip of his own coffee, and said that his name was Val, that he knew of her UFO experiences, and that he was here to help her. The fact that Sandy was hardly someone who broadcasted her UFO experiences far and wide (quite the opposite, in fact; she has never written, blogged, or spoken about her alien encounters publicly) immediately made her wonder how, exactly, her mysterious visitor seemingly knew so much about her. The answers soon came tumbling out.

Val proceeded to tell an amazing, albeit brief, story. Mason's late father worked in the Pentagon in the 1980s in the field of counter-intelligence and, according to Val, had been carefully groomed and, as a result of his work, had been exposed to the deepest UFO secrets of the U.S. Government, including the history of human–ET interaction. That led her father to have a face-to-face encounter with an extraterrestrial in 1987, claimed Val, somewhere in the depths of Nevada. This encounter was not with one of the black-eyed, diminutive Greys, but with an entity that looked entirely human. That entity, Sandy Mason was told by her fellow coffee-drinker in Starbucks, was one Valiant Thor. Val continued that it was no coincidence both Sandy and her father had deep connections to the UFO phenomenon. It was a generational thing said Val, enigmatically, and without any degree of elaboration.

Mason, in a somewhat ironic situation, was actually already aware of the Stranges-Thor saga, having read *Stranger at the Pentagon* while in her late teens some two decades earlier. When Mason pointed out to the man opposite her that he appeared to be not more than a few years older than her at the very most and, therefore, could not have worked with her father 30 years earlier, Val opened a leather satchel he had with him and pulled out a much worn copy of *Stranger at the Pentagon*. In silence, he turned to a page that showed a photo of Valiant Thor, pointed to the picture, and passed it to Mason. She sat, chilled and dumbstruck by the fact that the face that jumped out of the pages of Frank Stranges' book and the one directly opposite her were undeniably identical. Yes, the clothes were different: in Stranges' book, Thor was dressed in a dark suit and tie. In 2012, however, he was wearing a black T-shirt, black jeans, and black combat boots. The slicked-back hair of the 1950s was gone too, replaced by a slight spiky style. But, it was clearly the same person. Or, maybe more correctly, it was the same ET.

Mason, who was quickly plunged into a state of shock—to the point where for a few minutes she felt decidedly light-headed and clammy—could only listen in silence as Thor told her an amazing story. Despite his unchanged appearance (the clothing and the hair aside), Thor quietly informed Mason that he and his kind had been working with high-ranking U.S. military, government, and intelligence officials since the 1950s. The alliance, as Thor described it, was an uneasy one. Thor's people wished to see us, the human race, develop; but their concern was that we are a highly violent and dangerous species, hence the careful selection of certain people who could help steer us in the right direction. Both Mason and her father, said Thor, were part of that process, although, rather frustratingly for Mason, Thor would elaborate no further on the matter of how exactly that steering process was likely to play out.

Immortality and Valiant Thor

Thor was, however, willing to answer questions on one issue. It was an issue that, almost inevitably, was bound to surface. Mason wanted to know why Thor looked exactly as he had back in the 1950s and 1960s. The human-looking alien first offered what Mason described as a strange and unsettling grin and then said something notable. It concerned something that was one of the main bones of contention between the Space Brothers and the U.S. Government.

There was, said Thor, a highly classified program within the U.S. Army that was hard at work trying to crack the alien secrets of immortality. And it had been doing so, wholly unsuccessfully, since the early 1970s. Thor and his people knew all about the project, but were one hundred percent unwilling to share their secrets due to the likelihood that those secrets would almost certainly be misused by an elite. Thor's race wished to see everyone benefit from those same secrets, but only when the time was right. Thor made it clear that, unfortunately for us in the early part of the 21st century, that time is perceived as being nowhere near soon yet.

Thor did, though, make a strange statement that may have revealed more than he intended. Or, maybe, he knew *exactly* what he was doing. Mason was told something along the lines of: "One day, your people will drink from the same cup as us, and your lives will not end" (Redfern, 2015).

The reference to drinking from the same cup clearly provokes imagery of the mysterious liquid that kept the Count of St. Germain young, of Indian Amrita and the Devas, and of the ambrosia of the Greek "gods," as well as the curious substances given numerous contactees and abductees, and as demonstrated by Joshua Cutchin. It may even recall the matter of White Powder Gold, too.

With the issue of immortality brought to a swift end, Thor stood up and said his goodbyes. As if anticipating that Mason would want to keep the conversation going, Thor assured her that she would hear from him one more time. "Hear from" proved to be the correct words.

The Night Caller

Around eight or nine days later, shortly after midnight, Mason received a phone call on her landline. The caller ID read "Private Caller." Somewhat concerned to get a call at such a late hour, she picked up the receiver and said "Hello?" (ibid.).

"Hello, Sandy," said the familiar voice. "It's Val; Val Thor," he added, in "Bond, James Bond"-style (ibid.).

Mason was hoping for far more than she got. But, even so, the brief conversation was eye-opening. According to Thor, he had made contact with 14 other abductees in California all within the confines of Starbucks coffee-shops, rather curiously, and during the course of the past week. He had similarly informed all of them of their roles in the process that lay ahead. Once again, and as Mason listened, Thor made a reference to taking a drink from the same cup, something which later made Mason wonder if the reason for Thor choosing coffee-shops was subtly symbolic: sitting and conversing over one very popular drink, while briefly discussing another mysterious cocktail that many would dearly love to get their hands on. Perhaps this relates to precisely the kind of symbolism described by Joshua Cutchin.

Although Sandy Mason never saw nor heard from Valiant Thor again, she remains confident that, one day, the next step in her interaction with immortal aliens will come to the fore and her questions of the "Why me?" variety will be answered.

Behind Closed Doors

One final thing on this issue: the story told to Mason by Thor echoes a very similar one I received in 2012—the very same year in which Mason had her encounter. It was all focused on a hush-hush program that was said to be run out of a particular facility in Utah, which may very well have been the Dugway Proving Ground, the chemical- and biological-warfare-based work that is shrouded in overwhelming secrecy. It was a program that allegedly began in 2003 and was prompted by the discovery of certain, unspecified, ancient things in Baghdad after the invasion of Iraq began—an issue that will be addressed to a far greater degree in the next chapter.

The project had at its heart something both amazing and controversial. It all revolved around nothing less than attempts to bring the human aging process to a halt—and maybe even *to reverse it*. This was, however, a very unusual program in the sense that it didn't just rely on modern-day technology and medicine. That may sound odd, but bear with me and I'll explain what I mean by that.

Yes, the program had a number of brilliant scientists attached to it, but it was also populated by biblical experts, historians, and archaeologists who were quietly contracted, hired, and subjected to grim nondisclosure agreements. The quest for the truth of immortality was to a very significant degree not based around the present or the future, but on the *distant past*. Much time was spent digging into accounts of none other than Manna from Heaven and the controversies surrounding what has become known as White Powder Gold, the Bread of Presence, and Amrita.

All of these have several things in common: (a) they have ancient origins; (b) they have to be ingested; (c) they have the potential to offer perfect health; and (d) they promise never-ending life. Of course, it must be stressed that is what legend, mythology, and ancient religious texts tell us. Actually *proving* that these mysterious "things" exist and also proving they can do what we are told they can do is a *very* different matter. So, I did what I always do in these situations, which is to listen very carefully to what the relevant person has to say. True or not, the story was pretty incredible.

Deep underground, scientists, who had spent much of their working lives striving to understand why exactly the aging process occurs as it does, were sat next to biblical experts who were deciphering and interpreting ancient texts on the aforementioned life-extending, digestible substances. Military personnel, who were dutifully ensuring the program ran under the strictest levels of security and safety, rubbed shoulders with modern-day alchemists, who were striving to crack the White Powder Gold conundrum. And learned souls in the fields of none other than ancient astronauts, the Bible's legendary giants, and the Anunnaki crossed paths with demonologists.

The story continued that at least as late as 2010, absolutely no progress had been made beyond adding to the lore and legend that surrounds tales of immortality and massive life spans in times long gone. Rather ironically, the fact that I was told the project was a complete failure added credibility to the story—for me, at least, it did. To me, it sounds *exactly* like the kind of off-the-wall program that significant amount of dollars might be provided to, in the event that it just might one day offer something sensational and literally life-changing. That the source of the story specifically *didn't* spin some controversial and conspiratorial tale of a secret, ruling elite living forever was one of the things that makes me think there just might have been something to all this—and perhaps there still is. Also, that Sandy Mason's encounter and story occurred in the same time frame is, if nothing else, highly intriguing. One day, it just might be shown as life-altering and world-changing.

Selected by Extraterrestrials

This particular story is not quite over. After reading the following, many might say that it has scarcely begun. In 2015, a man named William Mills Tompkins wrote a book titled *Selected by Extraterrestrials*. If you think that the title is controversial, you should check out the subtitle: *My Life in the Top Secret World of UFOs, Think-Tanks, and Nordic Secretaries*. Tompkins' story is a deeply strange one. It's a story that concerns his secret knowledge of classified UFO research programs undertaken from the 1940s onward, clandestine space-based projects, and even covert assistance given to the U.S. military and government by so-called "Nordic"-looking extraterrestrials who, just like Valiant Thor, were all but indistinguishable from us. Hence the curious term "Nordic Secretaries," which appears in the subtitle of Tompkins' book. As you may already have deduced from those two words, Tompkins claimed to have worked alongside a band of beautiful, extraterrestrial women from the 1950s onward who subtly, and sometimes not so subtly, provided information, data, and concepts that helped the U.S. space program to proceed far quicker than it would have without their help (Tompkins, 2015).

Many might write off Tompkins' undeniably outlandish claims without a second thought as the ramblings of an old man, now in his 90s. Perhaps, they would be correct to do so. Yet, despite the controversial nature of his story, Tompkins has a highly credible background and is still razor-sharp of mind. He spent many years working for TRW Inc. on classified space-based projects, and spent much time with the movers and shakers in the Pentagon, the White House, and the world of U.S. intelligence. Tompkins, as a result, has supporters in high places. One of them is Robert M. Wood, PhD, who spent 43 years working in a senior position with Douglas Aircraft and its successors. Wood says:

> I first met Bill on November 24, 2009 when he summarized his life for a couple of hours. One of the things that excited me was that he had worked at Douglas Aircraft Company from 1950 to 1963, and I had worked there the summers of 1949, 1950, 1953 through April 1954 and then from January 1956 until retirement in 1993. He and I had not met each other during our six years of overlapping time because he was initially a draftsman working in Ground Support Electronics, with whom I rarely had contact since I was involved in aerodynamic and thermodynamic issues. Nevertheless, we both worked for many of the same VPs and I knew or had met nearly all of the people he referenced (ibid.).

In 2015, Robert Wood hired me to check out Tompkins' claims and to fact-check the material in his then-unpublished manuscript; I did so for approximately three months. One of the revelations that crossed my path was particularly intriguing. In the latter part of 2010, Tompkins had a very weird encounter in a Walmart in Oceanside, California. It eerily mirrors the Starbucks-based experience of Sandy Mason at a Simi Valley Starbucks two years later.

According to Tompkins, it was around 1:30 p.m. when, in his own words, "I spotted an expensively dressed, tall, blonde, vision that immediately reminded me of the first day I met Jessica, my Nordic alien secretary at Douglas, nearly sixty years ago." Jessica was one of the primary ETs that Tompkins claimed helped to advance the U.S. space program when it was still in its infancy. Tompkins continued that "She stopped and turned, facing me. With a sincere, deep, penetrating look, this vision said, 'My father is several levels above 32 Mason, and I'm going to help you with your book'" (ibid.).

They talked for around 10 minutes, after which the woman suggested to Tompkins that they meet the following afternoon "in the coffee lounge," something else which also paralleled Sandy Mason's experience with Valiant Thor. The meeting went ahead and coffee was drunk; however, something was clearly wrong, as the woman elected not to "help" after all. "It's impossible at this time," she told a puzzled Tompkins. She quickly vanished and was never seen again (ibid.).

Tompkins later mused: "I am totally at loss about this encounter. But this young lady appeared to be, and spoke with the authority of, a Nordic Naval commander and could have been related to Jessica, the Nordic girl I had as my secretary through the Apollo program at Douglas Missile & Space Systems in Santa Monica, California" (ibid.).

Many people would likely scoff at such stories. Yet, tales like those of Bill Tompkins and Sandy Mason absolutely abound. And there's an intriguing afterword to all this: in the wake of the publication of *Selected by Extraterrestrials*, three readers—all friends and colleagues—came forward claiming to have encountered Tompkins' alluring Jessica in both the Pentagon and the headquarters of the Department of Homeland Security; not way back in the 1950s, but back in 2011, no less. All three asserted that, based upon Tompkins's description of Jessica in his book, Jessica had not aged from the time in the early 1950s when she worked alongside Tompkins to 2011. *She was unchanging*, just like Valiant Thor who, like those Nordic secretaries, was also rumored to have held a position of prominence in the inner-sanctums of the Pentagon.

CHAPTER 12

Seeking the Secrets of Eternal Youth

On March 19, 2003, President George Bush appeared on television before the American people and the world to announce that war with Iraq had just begun. The president said:

> My fellow citizens: At this hour, American and coalition forces are in the early stages of military operations to disarm Iraq, to free its people and to defend the world from grave danger. On my orders, coalition forces have begun striking selected targets of military importance to undermine Saddam Hussein's ability to wage war. These are opening stages of what will be a broad and concerted campaign. More than 35 countries are giving crucial support from the use of naval and air bases to help with intelligence and logistics to deployment of combat

units. Every nation in this coalition has chosen to bear the duty and share the honor of serving in our common defense (Bush, 2003).

President Bush continued with the following words: "To all the men and women of the United States armed forces now in the Middle East, the peace of a troubled world and the hopes of an oppressed people now depend on you. That trust is well placed. The enemies you confront will come to know your skill and bravery. The people you liberate will witness the honorable and decent spirit of the American military. In this conflict America faces an enemy that has no regard for conventions of war or rules of morality" (ibid.).

Saddam Hussein, Bush explained, had

placed Iraqi troops and equipment in civilian areas, attempting to use innocent men, women and children as shields for his own military. A final atrocity against his people. I want Americans and all the world to know that coalition forces will make every effort to spare innocent civilians from harm. A campaign on the harsh terrain of the nation as large as California could be longer and more difficult than some predict and helping Iraqis achieve a united, stable and free country will require our sustained commitment. We come to Iraq with respect for its citizens, for their great civilization and for the religious faiths they practice (ibid.).

President Bush stressed that

We have no ambition in Iraq except to remove a threat and restore control of that country to its own people. I know that the families of our military are praying that all those who serve will return safely and soon. Millions of Americans are praying with you for the safety of your loved ones and for the protection of the innocent. For your sacrifice you have the

War comes to Iraq (U.S. Government, 2003, Wikimedia Commons).

gratitude and respect of the American people and you can know that our forces will be coming home as soon as their work is done (ibid.).

And the president closed his speech with the following words:

Our nation enters this conflict reluctantly, yet our purpose is sure. The people of the United States and our friends and allies will not live at the mercy of an outlaw regime that threatens the peace with weapons of mass murder. We will meet that threat now with our army, air force, navy, coastguard and marines so that we do not have to meet it later with armies of firefighters and police and doctors on the streets of our cities.

Now that conflict has come, the only way to limit its duration is to apply decisive force and I assure you this will not be a campaign of half measures and we will accept no outcome but victory. My fellow citizens, the dangers to our country and the world will be overcome. We will pass through this time of peril and carry on the work of peace. We will defend our freedom. We will bring freedom to others and we will prevail. May God bless our country and all who defend her (ibid.).

An Alternative Agenda

Though the war in Iraq most certainly provoked widely varying opinions on the part of the American people—with many supporting it and just as many being vehemently against it—no one can deny that it resulted in one very positive outcome: the end of the regime of the tyrant Saddam Hussein. And, as history has also shown, it was the end of Hussein himself, too. That Hussein was shown to have played no role at all in 9/11, however, led many observers and commentators to wonder why such a war was ever waged in the first place. Yes, a ruthless dictator was dead, but so were thousands of American troops and many more Iraqi civilians. And the real orchestrators behind the terrible events of September 11, 2001—the Saudis—were still free. No wonder, then, that the war provoked massive controversy and huge, public demonstrations all around the world.

There is yet another controversy surrounding the war in Iraq that begs our attention. In fact, it practically *screams* for our attention and rightly so, too. It's a controversy that suggests there were other reasons—beyond just ousting an undeniable, murderous oppressor—as to why the U.S. Government specifically chose to invade Iraq, rather than go after the likes of the Saudis, who are widely believed to have played a major role in 9/11.

One of those reasons is directly connected to the subject matter of the book you are reading. So the story goes, amid all of the chaos and carnage of the war in Iraq, a special, secret unit was dispatched to seek out certain priceless and ancient artifacts that had a direct bearing on two specific issues: (a) the presence of extraterrestrials in Iraq thousands of years ago, and (b) the secrets of longevity and immortality. Was there a secret agenda in Iraq? An agenda intended to try and ensure that a powerful elite achieved unending life? That may very well have been the amazing situation.

Trying to Protect the Past

On the matter of this particular issue—namely, that of a covert program run by a highly secret element of the Bush administration to seek out the secrets of immortality—there is the pillaging of the National Museum of Iraq, which is situated within the city of Baghdad. Even in the buildup to the war, a great deal of concern was expressed about what might happen to the massive numbers of priceless archaeological marvels housed at the museum. For example, in January 2003, just two months before the war began, Andrew Lawler, writing in *Science*, said that "a battle is already under way over how best to preserve the country's vast cultural heritage. At the center of the controversy is a group of wealthy and influential American antiquities collectors and curators with enough clout to wangle a meeting last week with U.S. Defense and State department officials" (Lawler, 2003).

That meeting was intended to ensure, one way or another, that those literally thousands upon thousands of ancient items were not destroyed or stolen as a result of bombing missions and/or looting. No one, as war loomed large, doubted that there might very well be at least *some* historical losses; that was, after all, one of the unfortunate hazards of war. Very few, however, anticipated the sheer, incredible scale of what actually happened: namely, the deliberate and systematic targeting of certain areas of the National Museum of Iraq by unknown figures; a select band of people who were clearly intent on getting their hands on certain items of, we might say, an interesting nature.

Nippur: The Gilgamesh Connection

Jim Marrs, one of the leading figures within the world of conspiracy-themed research, both quickly and very astutely realized that the war in Iraq had multiple agendas and secrets attached to it. One of those agendas being the quest to secure ancient items that might be traceable back to the likes of the immortal Anunnaki and to none other than the legendary, and immortality-seeking, King Gilgamesh, too. We'll return to Marrs shortly. In the meantime, it is worth noting a seldom discussed fact: that just one year before the turn of the 21st century, archaeological digs of a very notable and intriguing nature were well under way approximately just 100 miles outside of Baghdad.

The University of Chicago notes: "In the desert a hundred miles south of Baghdad, Iraq, lies a great mound of man-made debris sixty feet high and almost a mile across. This is Nippur, for thousands of years the religious center of Mesopotamia, where Enlil, the supreme god of the Sumerian pantheon, created mankind" (University of Chicago, 2014).

Enlil, of course, was in reality none other than one of the Anunnaki.

University of Chicago staff continue that Nippur was a place of deep significance from a political perspective, and also as a result of the fact that it became a location to which numerous ancient rulers and kings traveled to, including Babylon's Hammurabi, who was a noted warlord and the sixth king of the first Babylonian dynasty, and who ruled from 1810 to 1750 BC. Assyria's Ashurbanipal was another powerful figure who considered Nippur to be an important locale. He was a man who is perhaps most well known and remembered for having created the impressive Library of Ashurbanipal, a huge collection of priceless, old cuneiforms. That Nippur was seen by many as a deeply religious place meant that, fortunately for its inhabitants, it was rarely dragged into battles and turf wars of the kind that ravaged the likes of Babylon and Nineveh. And there is a very good reason as to why the area became of such deep interest as the 20th century came to an end, and as a new century—and a new war—began: Nippur has a link to King Gilgamesh, the demigod who tried in vain to become an immortal.

It should be noted that the area, which began to flourish around 7,000 years ago, played a major role in the history of our earliest cultures. It was no ramshackle collection of buildings, but a vast metropolis, replete with places of worship, market places, and buildings dedicated to the work of local government. In addition, it was a site at which literally thousands of ancient stories were chronicled on ancient tablets, one such story being that of Gilgamesh.

Back to the King Who Wanted to Live Forever

As for that 1999 dig, it was overseen by one Riyadh al-Douri, a noted expert in the field of ancient excavations. The world's media took a great deal of interest in the findings at Basmyiah, which is less than a two-hour-long drive from the city of Baghdad. Those same findings included not just toys and models of animals, but also what were intriguingly referred to as ancient weapons and a seal that showed the image of a very tall humanoid. That same, giant entity was believed by many historians to have been a rendition of none other than King Gilgamesh, who desperately sought the secrets of living forever, but who ultimately failed in his quest (as we have seen) and who was reputedly of a giant size.

In 2002, one year before the war began, even more amazing discoveries were made, including deep below the ground at Uruk, where what were described as the remains of ancient palaces, gardens, and huge walls were discovered. One of the team members, Jorg Fassbinder, said that the discovery amounted to "a Venice in the desert." The possible remains of Gilgamesh's tomb were also believed to have been found by the team on the Euphrates River ("Gilgamesh tomb believed found," 2003).

Looting, Pillaging, and Seeking the Secrets of Immortality

As all of this clearly serves to demonstrate, in the buildup to the war in Iraq, extraordinary discoveries were being made in very close proximity to Baghdad, many of them linked to King Gilgamesh and to the legends surrounding the powerful Sumerian god, Enlil. Or, rather, surrounding a powerful member of the Anunnaki. That so many of those Gilgamesh-connected artifacts made their way to the Baghdad-based National Museum of Iraq very possibly prompted what happened next; namely, in the early stages of the war, the massive looting of that very same museum. Just how extensively planned the pillaging was can be demonstrated by the words of a number of well-informed figures, ones who did their utmost to ensure the massive theft did not go by unnoticed or uninvestigated.

Robert M. Poole, at the Smithsonian Website, said: "All the looting at Baghdad's Iraq Museum had taken place by the time U.S. troops—engaged in toppling Saddam Hussein—arrived to protect it, on April 16, 2003" (Poole, 2008).

Tragically, the troops were only days late in preventing that same, widespread looting. It was on April 8 that the museum's staff were ordered to leave the museum, chiefly for their own safety. Although they were back barely four days later, the damage had already been done: more than 15,000 priceless items were gone, stolen and pillaged by, well, no one really knew who—largely as a result of the chaos and warfare that was exploding all across Baghdad. There was, however, a smidgen of light at the end of the tunnel: initial estimates suggested that the losses were well into six figures, which would have been almost unimaginable for those tasked with caring for the priceless items. Thankfully, that was not the case. Nevertheless, it was still a major disaster for museum staff, historians, and archaeologists. Dr. Donny George Youkhanna, who had previously held the position of Director-General of Iraq's various museums, made it clear that for the people of Iraq this was a disaster of significant proportions.

"It Didn't Have to Happen"

McGuire Gibson, of the University of Chicago, said something that many were thinking or, at the very least, strongly suspecting: that the plundering of the museum "was a very, very deliberate, planned action. They were able to obtain keys from somewhere for the vaults and were able to take out the very important, the very best material. I have a suspicion it was organized outside the country. In fact, I'm pretty sure it was" (Burkeman, 2003).

Dr. Donny George Youkhanna, of the museum itself, had his say on the matter too. He made no bones about his opinion: "I believe they were people who knew what they wanted. They had passed by the gypsum copy of the Black Obelisk. This means that they must have been specialists. They did not touch the copies" (Talbot, 2003).

The *American Free Press* made an important observation too: "Glass cutters not available in Iraq were found in the museum and a huge bronze bust weighing hundreds of pounds would have required a fork lift to remove it indicate that well organized professional cultural thieves were mixed in with the mob" (Marrs, 2006).

Then, there was this brief but important statement from *Business Week*: "It was almost as if the perpetrators were waiting for Baghdad to fall to make their move" (Talbot, 2003). Quite so.

On April 18, 2003, the UK's *Guardian* newspaper noted something intriguing; something that may have directly—and perhaps even deliberately—aided the looters in their unfortunately successful actions. Senior U.S. military officers confirmed that it had not taken any steps at all to prevent looting of the museum, or "to prevent the burning of the national library there, apparently causing the loss of priceless manuscripts centuries old. Efforts had been made to protect cultural sites from being targeted by missiles or caught up in ground fighting, *but not to shield them from looters* [italics mine]" (Burkeman, 2003).

The *Guardian* story was directly prompted by the controversial resignations of two central figures within the Bush administration. They were

Martin Sullivan, who, at the time, was the chairman of the President's Advisory Committee on Cultural Property, and Gary Vikan, who was a member of that same committee. Both men were utterly outraged by the situation and the widespread theft of priceless, millennia-old items. Sullivan, who had held the position of chairman for eight years before he quit, made no bones about the situation and came straight to the point: "It didn't have to happen. In a pre-emptive war that's the kind of thing you should have planned for" (World Revolution, 2003).

Vikan, who was the director of Baltimore's Walters Art Gallery, made his opinion very clear, too: "If we understood the value of Sumerian cuneiform tablets to our past, as we do with oil getting us somewhere in our cars, I don't think this would have happened" (Brown, 2003).

Perhaps the most important person in this entire, weird saga was Colonel Matthew Bogdanos of the U.S. Marine Corps. It's pretty much all thanks to the sterling work of Colonel Bogdanos that we know of the extent of the massive pillaging, and of the clearly well-coordinated way in which it was undertaken. The colonel said in 2004: "You have the public gallery from which originally forty exhibits were taken. We've recovered eleven. Turning to the storage rooms, there were about 3,150 pieces taken from those, and that's almost certainly by random and indiscriminant looters. Of those, we've recovered 2,700" ("Conversations: Building Trust in Iraq," 2004).

As positive as this reclamation certainly was, the U.S. military acknowledged that numerous items of both historical and archaeological importance remained missing. Into whose hands they had fallen was anyone's guess. Nevertheless, Colonel Bogdanos suspected that some kind of inside job was almost certainly afoot. He considered it beyond unlikely that the thefts were merely random events. He was sure that whoever the thieves were, they had personal and detailed information on the layout of the museum and where certain items were stored and contained. All of which leads us back to the work and startling conclusions of Jim Marrs.

"The Anunnaki Left Behind Some Very Hi-Tech Apparatus"

Marrs states: "The search for weapons of mass destruction that precipitated such a hurried rush into Baghdad may have concerned the many rare antiquities, to include perhaps ancient technologies, that comprise the heritage of Iraq" (Marrs, 2011).

Such issues were also addressed by Dr. Michael E. Salla of the Australian National University in Canberra. Salla said, in 2002, that "competing clandestine government organizations are struggling through proxy means to take control of ancient extraterrestrial (ET) technology that exists in Iraq" (2003).

Len Kasten says of Salla that he is of the opinion that certain nations including France, Germany, Russia, and the United States "have been aware that the Anunnaki left behind some very hi-tech apparatus, and possible weaponry, when they abandoned the earth around 1700 BC, and that Saddam Hussein had been getting assistance from Russian, German and French archaeological teams for years, in an attempt to unravel, and perhaps reverse-engineer this apparatus."

Kasten adds that some secret organization—comprised of individuals from the above nations, and working alongside Iraqi experts—might very well be able to understand and even replicate any potential extraterrestrial artifacts found during the plundering of Baghdad. Kasten has also commented on the possibility that, one day, the Anunnaki may return to our planet. And, should that be the case, then the possibility of doing a kind of deal with these ancient ETs might very well be on the cards. Kasten also notes that Salla believes that some sort of incredibly well hidden body of powerful figures—a New World Order, one might say—is at the heart of the attempts to secure and understand the ancient technologies that may exist in and around Baghdad.

Did the war in Iraq serve, in part at least, as a cover to allow for certain highly classified operations to go ahead? Did those same operations revolve around a quest to seek out the secrets of immortality and the Anunnaki? As controversial as such questions undoubtedly are, the combined threads in this strange saga suggest strongly that this is *exactly* what was afoot. The biggest question that still remains unanswered, of course, is: did they—whoever they may be—succeed? Maybe so; as we'll see later, there is further evidence suggesting the U.S. Government may know a great deal about the issue of immortality and aliens, both ancient and modern.

Perhaps the biggest tragedy in this story is the long-term impact the looting had. Exactly 10 years after the mysterious affair, *Archaeology* magazine said: "a new generation of Iraqis has grown up without any access to the impressive network of museums across the country that were once crowded with schoolchildren. They know little of their ancient past. Many Iraqi politicians today have a bent toward Islamic fundamentalism that is no friend to secular archaeology" (Lawler, 2016).

Another side effect of the plundering of the museum is that many American archaeologists—who had previously undertaken groundbreaking work in Baghdad and its immediate surroundings—are now no longer welcome. That much has been made very clear by Liwaa Semeism, the minister of tourism, who has the last word on the activities of the State Board of Antiquities. He makes no bones about the fact he is against outsiders coming into the country and excavating the old landscape.

Clearly, there is a great deal more to this story; data that, almost certainly, remains under lock and key and far out of the hands of the media, the public, and the archaeological community. Nevertheless, I strongly suspect we have not heard the last of the mysterious looting of the National Museum of Iraq. Should the full story ever come tumbling out, it may well reveal to one and all that the war in Iraq did indeed have a covert agenda; namely, one designed to uncover ancient, Anunnaki-created technology that just might allow a powerful and dangerous elite to live forever.

CHAPTER 13

"Containers" of Souls

Most of the world's religions teach that the human soul is immortal. It is a belief that extends back to the very earliest years of human civilization. It's most intriguing, therefore, to note that in today's world of alien abductions a great deal of attention is focused upon the human soul. Not so much by UFO investigators, per se, but by the extraterrestrials themselves. The big question, of course, is: why? It's a question that quickly leads us down some very controversial pathways and even deeper rabbit holes, as we shall soon see.

Although the UFO phenomenon surfaced in spectacular fashion in the summer of 1947, it was not until the early part of the 1960s that the concept of alien abductions started to significantly develop in the minds of the collective UFO research community. Certainly, there were a few earlier cases—the highly controversial October 16, 1957, kidnapping of Antônio Vilas-Boas, in São Francisco de Sales, Brazil, being the most notable example. The bizarre nature of the experience, how-ever, which involved Vilas-Boas having wild sex with a human-looking extraterrestrial woman, led many overly conservative UFO investiga-tors of the day to dismiss it, perhaps due to nothing more than embar-rassment and a lack of open minds on their part. What could not be denied or buried, though, was the September 19, 1961, encounter of Betty and Barney Hill. The story is so well known that I'll provide just the briefest of summaries.

On the night in question, the Hills were driving home to Portsmouth, New Hampshire, after holidaying in and around Niagara Falls. It was at roughly 10:30 p.m. that Betty and Barney saw a strange light in the sky, one which did not appear to be evidence of an aircraft, at least not of any known type of regular aircraft. The Hills had with them a pair of binoculars and, as the light began to perform unusual maneuvers, they soon realized that it was some form of structured vehicle. As they passed through New Hampshire's White Mountains, which were largely free of other vehicles at the time, the object came very close to the ground to the extent that Barney, who was behind the wheel, was forced to bring the car to a quick halt. So near was the object, said Barney, he could see close to a dozen humanoid enti-ties peering out of a series of portholes that encircled the UFO. What reportedly happened next is highly controversial.

The Hills experienced a degree of what has since become known in Ufology as "missing time." In the days and weeks ahead, the pair had vague memories and nightmarish dreams, suggesting they had been taken on board the craft and subjected to a number of intrusive medi-cal experiments, including—they suspected strongly—some relative to the issue of human reproduction. Barney, for example, was made to ejaculate and a sperm sample was taken. Such was media and even U.S. military attention given to the affair, it led author John Fuller to pen a full-length book on the case, *The Interrupted Journey*, which was published in 1966.

The Abduction Epidemic Begins

In the years that followed, more and more high-profile abductions were reported, including the December 3, 1967, experience of police officer Herbert Schirmer. He was taken on board a UFO at Ashland, Nebraska, in the early hours of the morning in question and experienced missing time. Six years later, the U.S. media gave a great deal of coverage to the kidnapping of Charles Hickson and Calvin Parker by non-human entities. They suffered missing time and deep trauma while fishing on Mississippi's Pascagoula River on the night of October 11, 1973. The scenario was a typical one: invasive procedures undertaken by what were perceived to be ETs. Then, in November 1975, Travis Walton was abducted while working in Arizona's Apache-Sitgreaves National Forest. Such was the interest in the Walton case that in 1993 it became the subject of a big-bucks Hollywood movie, *Fire in the Sky*, starring D.B. Sweeney and James Garner, the latter of *The Rockford Files* fame.

It was, however, the 1980s that really saw the alien abduction phenomenon soar to previously unheard of heights. In 1981, Budd Hopkins' book on the subject, *Missing Time*, was published. Six years later, Whitley Strieber's *Communion* became a huge hit to such an extent that it reached number one on the *New York Times*' bestseller list. Indeed, one could make a solid argument that *Communion* quickly went from being a book to a veritable *phenomenon*. The insertion of John E. Mack in the controversy in the early 1990s gave the subject even more publicity, chiefly due to the fact that Mack was nothing less than a Harvard professor. As a collective result, alien abductions became major news. They are *still* major news for UFO investigators, albeit not quite to the extent they were in the 1980s and the early to mid-1990s.

A study of most publications on alien abductions demonstrates that the vast majority of observers, authors, and researchers of the phenomenon believe that what is taking place is a huge, secretive program to reap human DNA, eggs, sperm, and genetic materials. The reason: the so-called Greys are on a disastrous physical decline. They're slowly dying. As a means to try and save their civilization, they are reliant on using us as unwitting, and largely unknowing, donors. That's *us*, by the way. There is, however, another aspect to all of this. It's a deeply sinister aspect, too. Namely, it's the deep interest shown by the abductors in the immortal, human soul. Many abduction researchers ignore this issue. However, whether they do so due to a sense that the issue is too far out, or because it's an unsettling and potentially terrifying aspect remains debatable. Others, however, do not ignore it.

Life-Everlasting, Recycled Souls, and the "School"

When Whitley Strieber's *Communion* was published in 1987, it became a huge hit. It was a hit not just with the UFO research community, though, but with entire swathes of the public too. Even the mainstream media paid the book a great deal of attention, in part due to the fact that Strieber was already a very successful writer of atmospheric, thought-provoking horror fiction. His 1978 novel, *The Wolfen*, for example, was made into a successful movie in 1980. The massive attention shown to *Communion* was something that Ufologists had seldom seen before, *if ever*. Largely, the UFO community speaks to itself and to no one else. Strieber changed all that, and practically almost overnight. And Strieber changed something else, too.

Whereas most authors of books on the subject of alien abductions in the 1980s focused *solely* on the extraterrestrial scientists are here to steal our DNA angle, Strieber did not. Certainly, Strieber dug deep into this particular issue; however, he did not shy away from some of the far more controversial aspects of his own experiences with what he termed not aliens or extraterrestrials, but as the Visitors. It was a term Strieber used for a very good reason: he was not at all sure that his captors were alien—in the way we interpret the word, at least. Perhaps, he suggested, they represented something so strange that they are completely beyond our current comprehension. As Strieber noted, the

Visitors had a deep interest in the human soul; that one solitary part of us which, billions believe, never dies.

Not long after *Communion* hit the bookshelves, Strieber revealed that as a result of the phenomenal number of letters that had reached him, he was able to definitively state that the human soul was inextricably linked to the abduction puzzle. In his 1988 book *Transformation*, which was a direct follow-up to *Communion*, Strieber related a number of traumatic encounters involving abductees who felt that the Visitors/Greys had the ability to extract the immortal, human soul from the physical body. Not only that, they did so on numerous, regular occasions.

Strieber received a response from the Visitors that offered an explanation for their connections to the soul. They told him two things: first, that they recycled souls, and second, that the Earth is akin to being a school, one in which we are learning, growing, and evolving with every subsequent recycling. It's a scenario that provokes imagery of some huge, bizarre factory, unendingly dispatching old souls into new bodies in almost conveyor-belt-style fashion. Perhaps, that's *exactly* what is afoot—albeit in a very strange, near-unfathomable fashion that we have yet to come to grips with or even understand.

John Philoponus, born in Alexandria in 490 and a theologian, believed that the soul does not retain the memories of the deceased person (or persons) it once inhabited. Perhaps, that is indeed the case. Maybe, if Strieber's Visitors were being honest with him, when we're recycled into a newborn baby the soul lives on, but the memories of our past existences do not. In that sense, we may have *already* achieved immortality, but—in a strange state of deep and cruel irony—we don't know it because the slate is constantly being wiped clean every 80 or 90 years.

And Strieber was not the only one who came to realize that the alien abduction phenomenon was much weirder than most had imagined—maybe even weirder than most *could* ever imagine. One of them was the aforementioned Harvard-based Professor John E. Mack.

Echoing Strieber's words to a notable degree, Mack said that of the many and varied abductees he had helped and counseled, some felt that the entities they encountered were nothing less than soul-stealers. In his *Passport to the Cosmos* book, Mack described the story of an alien abductee named Greg. In Mack's own words, "Greg told me that the terror of his encounters with certain reptilian beings was so intense that he feared being separated from his soul. 'If I were to be separated from my soul,' he said, 'I would not have any sense of being. I think all my consciousness would go. I would cease to exist'" (Mack, 1999).

In some respects, Greg's words echo those of John Philoponus and the latter's beliefs that the soul, when recycled, does not retain the consciousness and memories of the person it previously inhabited.

"A Battlefield for Men's Minds and Souls"

It's hardly surprising, taking into consideration the soul-stealing angle of the abduction phenomenon, that some researchers have suggested that the Visitors are far less extraterrestrial-based and far more demonic in nature, as in *literally*. One of the most vocal and visible figures in this area is Tom Horn. He provides the following: "Demonology is not just another crackpot-ology. It is the ancient and scholarly study of the monsters and demons who have seemingly coexisted with man throughout history . . . The manifestations and occurrences described in this imposing literature are similar, if not entirely identical, to the UFO phenomenon itself" (Horn, 2011).

Horn has noted that those said to be in the throes of demonic manipulation present identical symptoms to those who have experienced profound UFO encounters, such as alien abduction and face-to-face experiences with ETs. Horn also notes that demons allegedly have the ability to shapeshift and take on just about any guise they please. He also reveals that the seemingly baffling ability of the so-called

Greys of Ufology to walk through doors and walls is also mirrored within the domain of demonology, too.

Then there is the saga of a man named Howard Menger, a well-known member of that elite club known as the contactees. They're the ones who maintain they have been contacted—sometimes in person, and on other occasions in a mind-to-mind situation—by benevolent "Space Brothers" from far-away worlds. In the mid-1950s, so Menger claimed, his allegedly alien friends told him that not only were there positive and negative non-human entities right here on Earth, but that our planet was a "battlefield" for nothing less than *"men's minds and souls* [italics mine]" (Menger, 1959).

Moving on, in October 1973, a significant UFO encounter occurred in the night sky of Mansfield, Ohio. It involved the crew of a U.S. Army Reserve helicopter that briefly witnessed at *very* close quarters a large, gray-colored, cylinder-shaped object. In the wake of the encounter, something very strange happened: the crew was quietly contacted by official sources that asked a lot of intriguing questions that are central to the theme of this chapter.

Sgt. John Healey, one of the crew members, later said: "As time would go by, the Pentagon would call us up and ask us: 'Well, has this incident happened to you since the occurrence?' And in two of the instances that I recall, what they questioned me, was, number one: have I ever dreamed of body separation? And I have. I dreamed that I was dead in bed and that my spirit or whatever, was floating, looking down at me lying dead in bed" (Zeidman, 1979).

Then there is the intriguing story of Paul Inglesby, the author of *UFOs and the Christian*. UFO researchers Dr. David Clarke and Andy Roberts recorded the following: "In 1938, while serving with the Royal Navy under Lord Mountbatten, [Inglesby] contracted a tropical disease and was left dangerously ill for three months. During this time he underwent a 'devastating spiritual experience,' during which he saw visions of a future atomic war and demonic forces controlling space ships and nuclear weapons" (Clarke and Roberts, 2007).

As Inglesby himself noted on this unsettling affair, "not only did I witness future events, in a mental telepathic sort of way, but throughout the whole of this time *a battle was raging for possession of my soul*'" (ibid.).

Back to Strieber

One of those who took a great deal of interest in Whitley Strieber's experiences and his book *Communion* was a writer named Ed Conroy. Conroy even wrote his own, impartial, book on Strieber and his encounters, *Report on Communion*, which was published in 1989. In the book, Conroy touched upon the death of Strieber's father, of which Strieber had a vision.

Conroy observed that it was experiences like that one which "led Strieber to speculate that perhaps the 'visitors' have a direct relationship with the world of human souls. It was enabling him to release guilt feelings about not having been present for his father's death." When Conroy asked if Strieber felt the Visitors may even have been somehow responsible for his father's passing, Strieber replied: "That did cross my mind and it was a terrifying and deeply disturbing thought" (Conroy, 1989).

Ishtar, the Visitors, and a Picture Paints a Thousand Words

In October 2001, Whitley Strieber posted a story to his Unknown Country Website titled "Temple of Ishtar Discovered." It states, in part: "Archeologists in Iraq have uncovered a temple dedicated to the goddess Ishtar in the ancient city of Babylon, 56 miles south of Baghdad. Ishtar was the goddess of love in Babylonia and Assyria. Under various names, the cult of the mother goddess spread throughout the ancient Near East" (Strieber, 2001).

As will be recalled from an earlier chapter, Ishtar, a Sumerian goddess of fertility, offered herself to King Gilgamesh who, at the time, was far more focused on immortality than he was on sex. It's surely no coincidence, then, that Strieber drew parallels between Ishtar and the female Visitor who appears in *Communion* and whose face stares eerily out of the cover of Strieber's hit book. Notably, in relation to the subject matter of the book you are now reading, Strieber sensed that the female entity before him was not just old, *but she was also incredibly ancient.*

The painting on the cover of *Communion*, which attracted so much attention, was the work of an artist named Ted Seth Jacobs. He recalls the process by which the artwork came to fruition. It was, he says, "painted in my small apartment on East 83rd St., in New York City.

The legendary goddess, Ishtar (BabelStone, 2010, Wikimedia Commons).

Whitley sat with me first for a drawing of the Alien. As I sketched, he would indicate how to change the portrait so that it would more match what he saw" (Crawford, 2012).

Jacobs explains it was a procedure that closely paralleled the kind of process followed by the police when trying to put together the facial image of a target of interest. The two worked closely, with Strieber describing the alien face and Jacobs following Strieber's lead. Interestingly, Jacobs reveals that during the process, the matter of the specific sex of the entity that appears was not discussed. Indeed, Jacobs suggested that perhaps the Greys don't even have genders, as we understand the term. Nevertheless, he did admit that there seemed to be a definite feminine quality to the finished work.

Still on the connection between Ishtar and Strieber, artist Michael Lombardi says: "This particularly struck me as my recent investigations of the ancients and roots of advanced human civilization make continued reference to intervention of 'the gods', with Ishtar being among them. Why would this individual reoccur, and with a similar 'divine' intervening approach?" (Lombardi, 2011).

Lombardi answers his very own question by stating that he finds it highly unlikely that tales such as those concerning Ishtar were nothing but stories. Rather, he suggests that such events at the dawning of human civilization really occurred, and that includes visitations from the likes of Ishtar.

Although we admittedly cannot conclusively prove it, this issue of Ishtar playing a role in the story of immortality-seeking Gilgamesh thousands of years ago, and Whitley Strieber making an Ishtar connection to his experiences today—experiences tied to the immortal soul—strongly suggest two things that are remarkable and incredible: (a) that the everlasting entities of Gilgamesh's era are still with us today; and (b) that soul-based immortality dominates the experiences of those caught up in the alien abduction phenomenon, both then and now.

Conspiracies and Immortality

Now, we come to the matter of what the U.S. Government—or, at the very least, a deeply buried and highly covert group within the governmental infrastructure—may know about the soul, immortality, and the recycling process upon which Whitley Strieber has focused so much of his attention. It's a very controversial story that comes from an equally controversial man. His name is Robert Scott Lazar. He is, however, far better known within the world of Ufology as Bob Lazar. According to Lazar, in late 1988 he spent a brief period of time employed at a highly secret and heavily fortified installation in Nevada code named S-4. It was a portion of the notorious Area 51. Lazar maintains that during the course of his several weeks spent at S-4, he got to see, handle, and even help to back-engineer a number of extraterrestrial spacecraft that an unknown element of the U.S. Government had acquired and under circumstances that Lazar was never made completely privy to.

Lazar also stated that, while at S-4, he was given the opportunity to review countless numbers of official documents on the long and winding history of the UFO/alien presence on our planet. One document in particular really stuck in Lazar's mind. It dealt with the early history of the human race, a history which suggested aliens had performed close to 70 genetic manipulations of the human species, and for who knows how many thousands of years—possibly *tens* and maybe *hundreds* of thousands years. Such was the level of concern that the personnel at S-4 had about this secret aspect of our history, the vast majority of all the relevant material was guarded with deadly force. It was not, however, being withheld for malicious or nefarious reasons. Rather, it was because no one knew how to break the disturbing news to the public without the revelation causing potential worldwide panic, shock, and disorder. So, an alternative approach was taken: the story was buried as deeply as was conceivably possible. This is not unlike the final scenes in the 1981 movie, *Raiders of the Lost Ark*, when the legendary Ark of the Covenant is hidden away from just about *everyone* in a huge warehouse.

As Lazar noted to Nevada-based George Knapp, of KLAS-TV, "there is an extremely classified document dealing with religion, and it's extremely thick. But why should there be any classified documents dealing with religion?" (Good, 1992).

Knapp wanted answers and he wanted them quickly. Lazar, after a fair bit of noticeable toing and froing, agreed to answer his own question: "We're containers. That's supposedly how the aliens look at us; that we are nothing but containers. *Maybe containers of souls* [italics mine]. You can come up with whatever theory you want. But we're containers, and that's how we're mentioned in the documents; that religion was specifically created so we have some rules and regulations for the sole purpose of not damaging the containers" (ibid.).

George Knapp was not the only person Bob Lazar told such a story to. Enter a man named Michael Lindemann, a UFO researcher, author, and futurist who secured a BA in psychology at Antioch University. In a recorded interview, Lazar made a short comment on the same controversial issue that he somewhat reluctantly discussed with Knapp:

> What they were talking about was the desirability of containers, and that the containers were not damaged. Now, people speculate on containers. Are they talking about containers of souls, something bizarre like that; or is it the opposite? Is the container the soul, and it contains the body? That's too far out really for me to grasp, but they were talking about the preservation of the containers, and how unique they are. Extremely, extremely unique. Very difficult to find (Lindemann, 1995).

When questioned by researcher Ralph Steiner, Lazar offered a similar reply: "I hate to repeat this stuff. I say this every time I mention it, because I have no other proof it's true, other than the fact that I read it;

and I always follow that up by saying, yes, everything I read about the propulsion system turned out to be fact" (Deschamps, 2016).

We'll end this chapter with the words of Ed Conroy: "To Whitley Strieber, the visitors are in essence agents of change, catalysts to personal evolution, *alchemists of the soul* [italics mine]. In a word, they are 'transformers'" (Conroy, 1989).

In the next chapter, we'll meet a man named Nigel Kerner. He has a very disturbing theory regarding how and why the Greys/Visitors are so immersed in the world of that which makes us already immortal—the human soul. It's a theory very different to that of Strieber, but no less paradigm-shifting and mind-blowing.

CHAPTER 14

The Greys: Desperately Seeking Souls

In the summer of 1997, one of the most controversial UFO-themed books ever written was published. Its title: *The Day After Roswell*. Ghosted by William Birnes, the editor of the now-defunct *UFO Magazine* and of History Channel's also defunct *UFO Hunters*, the book tells the story of one Philip Corso, specifically, Lieutenant Colonel Philip J. Corso, U.S. Army. Corso's story was both amazing and groundbreaking. But was it true? Although some in the field of Ufology embraced the story, many certainly did not, preferring instead to view the book as either government disinformation intended to confuse the truth of what really happened at Roswell, New Mexico, back in the summer of 1947, or nothing more than an elaborate and ingenious hoax designed to make money from the gullible and the "I want to believe" crowd.

According to Corso, he near-singlehandedly spearheaded a secret program designed to seed alleged alien technology and wreckage—recovered from the Foster Ranch, Lincoln County, New Mexico, by the U.S. Army Air Force's 509th Bomb Wing in July 1947—into the private sector. As a result of this clandestine operation, so Corso maintained, the United States was soon able to understand and even back-engineer at least *some* of the extraterrestrial materials. Fiber-optics, transistors, night-vision equipment, and computer chips were all, allegedly, a direct outgrowth of the extensive studies of the Roswell materials. But it's not so much the technology reportedly found at Roswell that we need to focus our attentions on; rather, it's the bodies of the beings allegedly found strewn around the crash site.

Extraterrestrials or Bio-Engineered Life-Forms?

Contrary to what the UFO community said or assumed, Corso never explicitly stated that the Roswell corpses were extraterrestrial. In fact, what he *really* said was quite the opposite. In Corso's story the so-called "Grey aliens" are actually created, built, or grown to perform specific tasks. As for the creators of the Greys, it was *they*, Corso maintained, who were the *real* aliens. Corso also said that, as far as he was aware, no one has ever seen the real aliens, only ever their black-eyed, large-headed worker-drones.

William Birnes said that Corso described the Greys as "an android or biological robot. He said it had no digestive system whatsoever and was connected electronically to the navigation controls of the spacecraft" (Birnes, 2012).

As for Corso himself, he stated: "perhaps we should consider the EBEs [Extraterrestrial Biological Entities] as described in the medical autopsy reports humanoid robots rather than lifeforms, specifically engineered for long distance travel through space or time" (Corso, 1997).

He expanded on this, outlining the profoundly weird nature of the Greys:

> While doctors couldn't figure out how the entities' essential body chemistry worked, they determined that they contained no new basic elements. However, the reports that I had suggested new combinations of organic compounds that required much more evaluation before doctors could form any opinions. Of specific interest was the fluid that served as blood but also seemed to regulate bodily functions in much the same way glandular secretions do for the human body. In these biological entities, the blood system and lymphatic systems seem to have been combined. And if an exchange of nutrients and waste occurred within their systems, that exchange could have only taken place through the creature's skin or the outer protective covering they wore because there were no digestive or waste systems (ibid.).

A similar scenario has been offered by The Hybrids Project that "these small grey beings are in fact biological workers. They appear to be fabricated workers which are the result of extremely advanced genetic manipulation. The Greys have succeeded in creating autonomous creatures, what we might call androids, who carry out mundane or dangerous tasks for the Tall Greys" ("Small Greys," 2015).

"What These Artificially Intelligent Entities Are Seeking Is Eternal Survivability"

Today, two decades after it surfaced, the strange story of Colonel Corso continues to divide the UFO research field. There is, however, a very good reason why I bring it up in the pages of this book. The idea that the Greys are not born, as such, but are grown or created has attracted the deep attention of a man named Nigel Kerner. He has developed an extensive and controversial theory that has a direct bearing upon matters relative to alien and human immortality. It's a theory detailed in Kerner's books, *The Song of the Greys* and *Grey Aliens and the Harvesting of Souls*—the latter being a book I provided a cover-blurb for.

Danielle Silverman is someone who undertook a great deal of research for Kerner and also someone who, in 2011, sent me a very illuminating statement for publication. She told me the following, which makes for fascinating reading. The immortal, human soul, she says, may well be "a derivational information field that comes out of a natural cadence that came into the Universe with the big bang. This field holds the power to maintain information in what [Kerner] called a morphogenetic electro-spatial field with an eternal scope of existence in whatever form circumstance allows" (Redfern, 2010).

Silverman suggests that the soul may actually be a form of mechanism for storing data. Keeping that scenario very much in mind, she notes that Kerner is of the view that if the Greys are indeed some kind of biological robot, then the soul may amount to "an analogue" of the very things that manufactured them in the first place (ibid.).

As Silverman also told me, Kerner suspects that the Greys are, in essence, biological machines; they are entities created and possessed of high degrees of intelligence, which are dispatched throughout the universe, effectively on exploratory missions. Kerner is keen to stress, however, that the Greys are not supermen or super-aliens. Rather, he believes them to be prone to their own equivalents of the wear and tear that affect all of us throughout our lives. The result is that the Greys are not invulnerable. They are quite the opposite, actually. And, given their mortality, they are driven to seek out, to understand, and even to try and find a way for themselves to have immortal souls.

Silverman explained to me that this latter issue gets right to the heart of the agenda of the Greys. Fully aware of the fact that they are not invulnerable to the rigors of time, the Greys are desperate to find a way to survive—and to survive forever. Though the Greys may, at the very least, carry certain DNA coding from the unknown extraterrestrial entities that created them in the first place, this does not allow them to survive eternally. But, via highly advanced genetic manipulation and exploitation of the human race, the Greys may manage to secure some kind of unending life, hence the near-endless number of reports of alien abduction and the reaping of bodily cells, DNA, sperm, and eggs that so many victims of such abductions report. Silverman suggests that the dark agenda of the Greys cannot work; that it's impossible for them to essentially create souls for themselves. But they appear not to be aware of that fact, which is why they endlessly attempt to do exactly that, and with no end in sight—as far as we can tell, at least.

Perhaps the most fantastic revelation that Silverman shared me with on this specific matter concerned Kerner's conclusion that the most profitable way to traverse the cosmos is via what he has termed Fields of Death. It's not as ominous as it sounds. Basically, Kerner has concluded that there is what we might call a zero-point area that exists in the specific spaces between atoms. This allows for incredible distances to be traveled in extraordinarily short periods of time—even allowing us to reincarnate on other worlds, in other solar systems, and maybe even in faraway galaxies. The Greys, seemingly, are aware of this post-death ability that we all apparently possess. In much the same way they are trying to perfect the ultimate soul to keep themselves alive, the Greys are doing their utmost to understand this afterlife ability to traverse the universe at incredible speeds and to replicate this, too.

As for Kerner himself, he provides us with the following: "I contend that there is something hugely meaningful about humanity, something virtual reality can never match, something artificial intelligence can never be programmed with. Words such as conscience, compassion, warmth, kindness, generosity, spontaneity, imagination, inspiration and creativity, give some hint as to what this something might be" (Kerner, 2010).

In terms of the specific nature of this mysterious something, Kerner believes it to be the soul. Kerner also concludes that the Greys are desperate to understand the nature of the soul, to the extent that they may even be able to replicate it in themselves, genetically. Doing so is the only way in which they can achieve unending existences, says Kerner. On this issue, he provides us with this:

> It is my thesis that the Greys, in contrast, are purely physical creations and thus completely subject to the entropic momentums that break down and decay physical states. They have no line of connection to any non-physical state that might lie beyond the physical mass soaked materiality of this universe, no "soul." Without this component, the Greys are completely subject to the breakdown momentums implicit within a physical universe. In my books I document alien genetic engineering at DNA level to evidence my theory these entities are attempting to "piggy back" our facility as human beings for eternal existence, hence their apparent fascination with the human reproductive capacity (ibid.).

This is something echoed by an alien abductee named Allison Reed. In an interaction with a Grey she learned something incredible. Reportedly, the Grey in question

> claims that he and his grey people are the result of genetic manipulation that some higher species, I guess, played God and mixed and matched and whatever. He and his people were created through a genetic alteration through a higher intelligence. I don't know what they were created for. But my understanding is that they were created for a purpose and, through the years, they weren't able to reproduce themselves anymore. From what he told me they didn't start this. They were a result, just like the hybrids are, from something else. From a higher intelligence (Jacobs, 2010).

And, now, the presently soulless Greys are on a mission to ensure that immortality is one day theirs. But only by understanding the nature of the human soul, figuring out what it is that gives us a soul-based immortality, and using advanced science and technology can they hope to achieve the one thing they so crave: never-ending life. Perhaps that's why, as Bob Lazar noted, the Greys view us not as humans, as people, or even as a species, but as containers. It's not our physical bodies that are the most important things to them. It's that ethereal, near-magical thing that is within all of us that they both want and need: the human soul, the key to living for all eternity.

CHAPTER 15

The Elohim, Cloning, and Living Forever

For some, they are a harmless bunch of eccentrics, ones whose minds are filled with odd beliefs concerning alien life and human origins. For others, they are a definitive cult. And, for more than a few, they are downright dangerous and reckless in their actions and proclamations. None of this, however, has prevented them from developing a massive, worldwide following. They go by the name of the Raelians—after their leader, Rael, who was born in Vichy, France, in 1946 with the much longer name of Claude Maurice Marcel Vorilhon. After a regular childhood and more than a bit of youthful, teenage rebellion in the late-1960s, Rael became a minor and brief celebrity in the field of French pop music. At the dawning of the 1970s, Rael gravitated to the world of racing cars and established his own magazine on the subject, *Autopop*. Two years later, specifically in December 1973, Rael's life took just about the strangest turn possible.

On December 13 and for no logical reason at all, Rael felt compelled to take a drive to Puy de Lasollas, which is situated near the capital of Avergne and the site of a dormant volcano. UFO researcher Dr. Jacques Vallee outlines what happened next: "The weather was foggy, overcast. [Rael] suddenly saw a blinking red light, and something like a helicopter came down and hovered two yards above the ground. It was the size of a small bus, conical on top. A stairway appeared, and a child-like occupant came out, smiling with a glow around his body" (Vallee, 2008).

The very human-looking extraterrestrial gave its name as Yahweh— also the name of the God of Israel—and entered into extensive dialog with the amazed and astonished Vorilhon. Such was the sheer level of data imparted to him, that Vorilhon wrote an entire book on his close encounter, titled (in English) *The Book Which Tells The Truth*. According to Vorilhon's cosmic source, the human race owed its origins to Yahweh's people: around 25,000 years ago, ETs visited the Earth and, via highly sophisticated DNA manipulation, gave birth to us, the human race.

Welcome to the World of the Elohim

The aliens were known as the Elohim, so Rael was advised, or those who came from the sky. This is not without a high degree of significance, as the following words demonstrate: "Elohim is one of three Divine Names by which the Creator is known as He creates. The creation account is probably the most difficult and most enigmatic passages in the Bible. It starts at the beginning and it doesn't really end. There are three stages upon which the creation unfolds" ("Elohim Meaning," 2016).

As for what exactly those three stages are, they can be explained as the period described in the Old Testament's Genesis 1:1 to 2:4. It's in this specific time frame that God is referred to as Elohim. From Genesis 2:4 onward, God's title is Yhwh Elohim. At least, that is, until we reach what are referred to as the Noah and Abraham Cycles, and which extend throughout the remainder of the Bible. It's in this particular period that God becomes known as Dabar yhwh or, as it translates, word of God.

The Raelians believe that during the early, burgeoning years of human development, the Elohim sent a number of ambassadors to our planet, chiefly as a means to try and ensure that early man lived a good and peaceful life. Among those ambassadors were such luminaries as Buddha, Jesus, and Moses. And those same Elohim had a firm plan in mind for Rael—a plan which has, ever since, pretty much dominated the rest of his life.

One day, Rael was told, the Elohim will return to the Earth and finally show themselves—and on a planet-wide scale, no less. Rael was specifically selected as their number-one on Earth to pave the way for the return of the ancient alien race. The first thing Rael was asked to do was to build an embassy for the aliens, and also to create a group to which others of a like-mind could gravitate. Its name is The Movement for Welcoming the Elohim, Creators of Humanity, or Madech in abbreviated form.

It was in September 1974 that things exploded big time for Rael. That was the month in which he held a major conference in the city of Paris, at which he told the story of his by now extensive encounters, and of the alien Elohim and their mission on Earth. It was a phenomenally successful conference, one that attracted more than 2,000 curious and excited attendees. Madech soon became the International Raelian Movement, and in no time the group went global. The rest, as the old saying goes, is history. The Raelians continue to thrive and even to attract worldwide attention, as we shall soon see, particularly so in relation to the matter of immortality and aliens.

Who Were the Elohim?

Before we get to the issue of extraterrestrials and life-everlasting, it's important to understand who the Raelians believe the Elohim to be. It's also important to note there are conflicting views on the nature of the Elohim. Back in 1908, Hiram Butler, the author of *The Goal of Life*, wrote:

> It was the Elohim that the Lord Jesus called his Father . . . The very first utterance of the Old Testament is, "In the beginning God [Elohim] created the heaven and the earth." The noun Elohim is in the plural form, and it would have been correct had the sentence been translated, "In the beginning the Gods created the heaven and the earth." Some authorities have ingeniously tried to evade the consequences of the plural noun in this case by explaining that it is a "plural of excellence." Others hold that it signifies a plurality of attributes or manifestations; but the fact stands out incontrovertibly that throughout is meant a plurality of individuals, and when we reach the 26th verse, we read that Elohim said, "Let us make man in our image, after our likeness" (Butler, 1908).

Moving on, let's take a closer look at the alleged extraterrestrial origins of the Elohim. In a 1997 interview with Zecharia Sitchin, UFO investigator Jordan Maxwell asked a pertinent question: "Were the Elohim the 'sons' of the sons of God, or were the Elohim the 'sons of God'?" (Maxwell, 1997).

It was a question to which Sitchin replied: "They were the Anunnaki. And it is their sons born on earth who married the daughters of Adam" (ibid.).

In other words, Sitchin's Anunnaki and Rael's Elohim are one and the same—which is interesting, given that Sitchin believed the Anunnaki to have achieved incredible life spans, whereas the Raelians claim that the Elohim have cracked the code that leads to immortality.

Of course, there is another explanation too, namely one that places the Elohim firmly in the camp of Hebrew teachings: "The word Elohim is the plural of El (or possibly of Eloah and is the first name of God give in the Tanakh: 'In the beginning, God (Elohim) created the heavens and the earth.' The name Elohim is unique to Hebrew thinking: it occurs only in Hebrew" (Parsons, 2016).

Now, let's see more of what the Raelians say about the Elohim. In the Raelians' own words, which they specifically refer to as *The Message*, "Thousands of years ago, scientists from another planet came to Earth and created all forms of life, including human beings, whom they created in their own image. References to these scientists and their work can be found in the ancient texts of many cultures" ("The Message," 2016).

The Raelians continue that that these ancient extraterrestrials—otherwise known as the Elohim—specifically utilized certain prophets to help educate and inform the people of Earth, and also to help with the careful development of civilization with certain, specific rules and regulations. Top of the list were warnings and messages to the human race that we should specifically avoid violence—war, murder, and so on—and have a deep respect for our fellow humans. In the very earliest of times, the Elohim reportedly allowed those same prophets to do just about all of their message-based work for them. As we progressed as a species, however, the Elohim elected to show themselves more and more, hence the wave of UFO activity that kicked off, big time, in the summer of 1947. It was this greater openness and visibility, say the Raelians, that led the Elohim to contact Rael himself in the 1970s and have him inform the world of their agenda and to construct an embassy in their honor.

Highway to Hell (or Heaven)? Hell, No!

We've seen how the Raelians have come to believe that the Elohim are the creators of the human species, the founders of just about all our major religions, and immortal entities from a faraway world. Now, it's time to see how and why the Raelians believe that we, too, may one day follow the Elohim down the road to life-everlasting. The story is, as one might guess, filled with controversy.

Given that most of our long-established religions believe in the existence of a soul or a life-force—one that lives on forever after our physical body dies—it may come as a surprise to many to learn that the Raelians have no belief in the soul at all. Their conclusion, based upon their reported contacts with the Elohim, is that whatever makes us who we are as unique individuals with equally unique characters winks out of existence at the time of bodily death. And that is *all* it does. For the Raelians, there is no afterlife. There is no Heaven. There is no Hell. And there is no Purgatory. Zoroastrianism's Paradise is a mere myth. The same goes for Buddhism's Nirvana and Bardo, and also for Hinduism's Moksha. What about the ancient Greeks' Hades? It's nothing but the equivalent of a fairy-story designed to frighten and control the populace. And the list goes on. As the Raelians see it, when the lights go out for each and every one of us, they go out forever. It's game over, irreversible, unending extinction. That is, however, unless one understands and has the ability to replicate the means by which the Elohim have managed to keep death's clutches at arm's length. It all revolves around not the soul, but the expanding science of human cloning.

The Science of Never-Ending Duplicates

Although cloning is a very complicated process, it has been concisely explained: "Cloning produces a new individual using only one person's DNA. The process is technically difficult but conceptually simple. Scientists remove the genetic material from an unfertilized egg, then introduce new DNA from a cell of the animal to be cloned." The result is that the cell then begins a process of splitting into completely new cells "according to the instructions in the introduced DNA" ("Group claims human cloning success" (2002).

The U.S. Government's National Human Genome Research Institute says of the cloning process that there are, specifically, three kinds of cloning that have been shown to work, and to varying degrees of success. Though they all fall under the banner of cloning, they are in fact significantly different. For example, what is termed gene cloning is designed to create duplicates of portions of DNA or of genes. Then there is reproductive cloning. Unlike gene cloning, the goal here is to create carbon-copies of an entire animal. And, finally, we have therapeutic cloning, which results in new tissue to take the place of decayed or degraded tissue, very often caused by serious disease and illness.

The Raelians firmly believe that the only way to achieve immortality is by creating a perfect clone of oneself. Massively increasing the speed by which the embryo becomes a baby, then a child, and finally an adult via the use of nanotechnology and futuristic, genetic manipulation will be the name of the game. Then, when the clone has reached maturity—not in 20 or 30 years, but perhaps in as few as four or five years—the mind, the personality, and even the memories of the original person will be transplanted into his or her clone. In theory, such a thing could continue ad infinitum. As the clone begins to age, another one is grown and the process of transferring those aforementioned memories and personality into the next, younger clone goes ahead, and then into the next, and the next . . . and the next. In theory, the process would allow for never-ending life at an age of one's personal choosing, and all the while without any need whatsoever for a soul or an existence in an ethereal, supernatural afterlife. If a conveyor belt of cloned duplicates is good enough for the Elohim, then it's certainly good enough for the Raelians too.

"The Law Does Not Define the Term 'Human Being'"

Regardless of which side of the fence one sits on, none can deny that just about everything said and claimed by the Raelians is steeped in controversy. And that includes the matter of human cloning—a process that is almost uniformly seen by the public, the medical community, and even governments as abhorrent and dangerously reckless. Christopher A. Pynes of Western Illinois University notes that: "The U.K. has a clear prohibition on reproductive human cloning, but works to keep laws current with and relevant to technological advances. The EU supports funding for embryonic stem cell research, but has banned human cloning" (Pynes, 2009).

Pynes adds that, on this particular issue, "The USA has a complex mix of state and federal regulations and interlocutors" (Pynes, 2009). Indeed, it does, chiefly due to the controversies surrounding abortion, stem cell research, and the overall issue of cloning in general.

The NCSL (the National Conference of State Legislatures) expands on the present situation in the United States. It notes that of all the U.S. states, 15 of them have specific laws governing cloning, and which for the most part, are designed to ensure that cloning procedures do not cross the line when it comes to what is deemed ethical—in terms of furthering science and medicine—and to ensure that we don't go down some highly controversial Dr. Frankenstein-like path, as we seek to perfect the cloning process.

In view of the words of both the NCSL and Christopher A. Pynes, it's hardly surprising that when, in 2002, a Raelian bishop named Brigitte Boisselier announced that cloning science had led directly to the birth of a baby, all hell broke loose. This is assuming, of course, that hell really exists, which the Raelians do not assume in the slightest. But we're getting a little ahead of ourselves here. To understand and appreciate the full story surrounding this unique baby, we have to go back to 1997.

The Bishop and the Clones

It was specifically in February 1997 that Rael created a body called Valiant Venture Ltd. Corporation (VVLC), and which oversaw a company known as CLONAID. Its purpose was to study and examine the feasibility of creating human life via the process of cloning which, the Raelians believe, allowed them to achieve immortality as we have seen. Thanks to significant financial input from a variety of investors, the company very soon had a headquarters in the Bahamas. It also had money to work with and goals to be achieved—very controversial goals, too, it should be noted. In no time at all, the world's media was hot on the trail of what was afoot in the domain of VVLC—as were senior government officials in the Bahamas, which is managed by the UK's Queen Elizabeth II, a governor-general, and a prime minister. It was one thing for VVLC and CLONAID to say they were going to study the science of cloning in the Bahamas. For the government of the Bahamas, however, its staff had visions of Dr. Frankenstein–style laboratories and secret facilities popping up all across the Bahamas' more than 700 islands and wreaking untold nightmarish havoc in the process.

CLONAID's staff reveal that at the same time it became clear to the Bahaman authorities what was afoot—and what else of a controversial nature that might be looming large on the horizon—a great deal of concern was also exhibited by certain factions of the media. Journalists made vocal observations suggesting that the cloning labs would be built and operated on the Bahamas, which, hardly surprisingly, deeply concerned the government. CLONAID's staff say that, while all of this was going on, the number of "serious potential customers had grown to more than 250 people! Therefore, during the year 2000, Rael decided to hand over the CLONAID project to Dr. Brigitte Boisselier, a Raelian Bishop, in order for her to start working on actually cloning the first human being with a team of well-trained scientists" ("History," 2009).

And start working they most assuredly did: in the heart of Las Vegas, Nevada. For the most part, everything was done quietly and behind the scenes. Although, it should be noted that American official-dom was far from happy with what was afoot in Sin City, as CLONAID admits. Indeed, halfway through 2001, certain U.S. authorities paid CLONAID a visit, and then another, and another. It was clear that someone in authority had major concerns as to what was going down in the world of cloning. We're talking about visits by staff from none other than the criminal investigations division of the Food and Drug Administration (FDA) to CLONAID's facility in Nitro, West Virginia. FDA staff were surprised to see that the lab was packed to the rafters with high-tech equipment, and all paid for by a man named Mark Hunt, formerly a West Virginian state legislator. Tragically, Hunt's son died in 1999 before he was even one year old. Hunt, still grieving, had decided to allow CLONAID to bring his son back—although the extent to which the clone would have been Hunt's son in both charac-ter and physicality was debatable. When approached by the FDA, Hunt agreed that if he were to go ahead with the cloning of his son, he would arrange for it to take place specifically *outside* of the United States.

The Controversy Heats Up

In December 2002, the world woke up to news that—depending on one's views—was either amazing or downright appalling and creepy. CLONAID claimed it had gone where many thought it *shouldn't*, and even more prayed it *couldn't*. On December 28, 2002, CNN ran a major article on the controversy. Fox News was quickly onto the story, too, as was the BBC. In no time at all, just about the entire world's media was reporting on the birth of what was claimed to be the first human clone.

Inevitably, a great deal of skepticism surrounded CLONAID's announcement concerning baby Eve, which came from none other than Brigitte Boisselier herself. Much of the skepticism was prompted by Boisselier's decision to remain decidedly tight-lipped on major portions of the story. For example, she flatly refused to reveal in which country the baby was born, brushed aside demands for the name of the mother (but did admit she was American), and would say very little about the father except that he was infertile, hence the need for Eve to have been cloned from her mother's DNA.

In a press conference held in Hollywood, Florida, Boisselier said that, "The baby is very healthy. The parents are happy. I hope that you remember them when you talk about this baby—not like a monster, like some results of something that is disgusting" (Dakks, 2002).

Concerns about Cloning

The parents may well have been happy. Not everyone was, though. Jonathan Moreno, an ethicist, was deeply concerned. He pointed out, correctly it's very important to stress, that when cloning processes were used on animals, the results were very often disastrous, with animals suffering from rapid aging, cancerous tumors, and issues of a neurological nature. Moreno added that, as far as this new development in human cloning was concerned, we were dealing with unchartered waters.

The reference to clones aging prematurely was deeply ironic, taking into consideration the fact that the Raelians are constantly seeking to achieve immortality. Make no mistake, many cloning experts fear that the process could cause more problems than it might solve. Back to the U.S. Government's National Human Genome Research Institute (NHGRI), the research of which paints a decidedly grim picture. It's a picture that is at distinct odds with the beliefs and claims of the Raelians.

The NHGRI says of the profound, potential hazards relative to cloning: "Another potential problem centers on the relative age of the cloned cell's chromosomes. As cells go through their normal rounds of division, the tips of the chromosomes, called telomeres, shrink. Over time, the telomeres become so short that the cell can no longer divide and, consequently, the cell dies" ("Cloning," 2016).

The NHGRI also noted that although all of this was very much in accord with the natural process of aging that affects cells, if the cells used to create the clone were taken from an adult, then the chromosomes of that very same adult might already be significantly aged, which could have a spiraling, knock-on effect for the clone to the point where the life span of the clone could be sorely limited. As a classic example of this, the NHGRI cited the case of Dolly the sheep, who was cloned in Scotland in 1996 at the Roslin Institute, a section of the University of Edinburgh. Despite the fact that a sheep like Dolly could have expected to have reached the age of 11 or 12, she barely made it past six, primarily due to the fact that she developed severe arthritis and damage to her lungs—all of which one would have expected to see in a much older sheep. Dolly was put to sleep on February 14, 2003.

Steve Stice, an authority on cloning and based at the University of Georgia, was concise in his words: "I'm hoping that it's not true" (Ritter, 2002).

Of course, much of the skepticism came from the fact that it was pretty much impossible to separate CLONAID from the Raelians, chiefly because Boisselier was a major figure in both camps. As the days and weeks progressed, the media pushed for more answers. Boisselier remained fairly quiet, however, beyond adding that Eve and her mother returned home on New Year's Eve, 2002. To date, and despite legal threats and even court cases, Eve's identity has still yet to be revealed. Nor have the names of the *additional* clones that are said to exist and which, CLONAID assures us, are doing just fine. Indeed, on January 6, 2003, *New Scientist* reported that Boisselier "told the BBC that her medical team had created *several hundred cloned embryos* [italics mine] before conducting ten implantation experiments. Two of these have led to live births, she says, with three more expected by the end of January" (McDowell, 2003).

And CLONAID is still standing by its conviction that immortality, via cloning techniques, is firmly on the horizon. The organization believes that it won't be long at all before highly sophisticated cloning techniques will allow us to "recreate a deceased person in an adult body, with all his past experiences and memories, allowing mankind to enter the age of immortality as it has been announced by His Holiness Rael, founder of Clonaid, in 1973 already after his contact with the Elohim, mankind's extraterrestrial creators" ("Godsend: The Movie, Clonaid: The Reality," 2009).

Time will tell. Maybe.

CHAPTER 16

The Science of Immortality

The issue of why we age, and ultimately and inevitably die, is a complex one. It can, however, be understood by looking at what is termed the "Hayflick Limit." It's explained by Zane Bartlett as follows: "The Hayflick Limit is a concept that helps to explain the mechanisms behind cellular aging. The concept states that a normal human cell can only replicate and divide forty to sixty times before it cannot divide anymore, and will break down by programmed cell death or apoptosis" (Z. Bartlett, 2014).

If, however, as all of the available evidence strongly suggests, ancient extraterrestrials cracked the code that led them to attain something we all deeply desire—everlasting life—then, surely, the biggest and most important question is: how did they achieve it? It's all but impossible for us to say with absolute certainty, given that the available evidence suggests such an amazing breakthrough was made countless millennia ago and on other, faraway, worlds too. That said, however, logic dictates that it was thanks to the likes of White Powder Gold, advances in extraterrestrial medicine, science, technology, and an understanding of DNA and its attendant complexities that opened the gates to immortality and kept those same gates open, permanently. How can we be so sure?

Put simply, we are now following the very same path that the likes of the Anunnaki may have walked hundreds of thousands of years ago. In other words, scientists, geneticists, and doctors are now seriously looking at the idea and the real feasibility of extending human life spans to radical degrees and, possibly, even to the point where one day death just might be a thing of the past. By studying our very own burgeoning immersion into the strange and potentially life-changing realm of immortality, we just may gain some degree of notable understanding of how our alien visitors did likewise in the distant past.

The ancient people of Egypt, India, the Middle East, and Greece recognized that, unlike mere mortals, the gods lived forever. Those same people dearly—perhaps even desperately—wished to have that same immortality, or at least, incredibly long life spans, bestowed upon them. In some cases, that may have been exactly what happened, and particularly so with regard to the likes of Adam, whose age at his death was said to have been 930, and Methuselah, who allegedly lived to the age of 969 years. It may have happened to King Gilgamesh too, the powerful Sumerian demigod who, it's claimed, ruled over the Babylonian city of Uruk for more than a century.

It must be said that despite the passing of thousands of years, very little has changed: in the same way that Gilgamesh—realizing that time was running out—craved immortality all those millennia ago, we, today, are doing all we can to keep the icy clutches of the Grim Reaper from taking us. It is research that is heading in some decidedly alternative directions.

From Man to Machine

It's intriguing to note that Whitley Strieber, the author of the phenomenally successful 1987 book, *Communion*, has suggested that the so-called Greys are not all they appear to be. They may be far more. Or, paradoxically, they just might be far less. Strieber opines that the Greys may have the ability to exist in a non-physical, ethereal, soul-based state of immortality. He doesn't stop there, however. Strieber also suggest that the dwarfish, large-headed bodies of the Greys (reported in numerous alien abduction cases) may actually be akin to diving suits, specifically of the kind that we use when we wish to leave our land-based environment and head into the depths of a very different environment: the oceans of our world. In other words, and as Strieber sees it, the bodies of the Greys may actually be highly sophisticated, biological robots—bodies that are only used when the immortal life-forces of the Greys need to temporarily leave that ethereal realm and operate on a physical, three-dimensional plane. As Strieber concisely suggested, we're talking about something akin to biological robots into which souls may be implanted or even removed, as circumstances dictate—something which makes the diving suit comparison work very well.

Not Quite Human Anymore

Mac Tonnies had thought-provoking words to say on this very matter:

> Given the vast number of out-of-body and near-death experiences, I find it difficult to reject the prospect of "nonlocal" consciousness; perhaps a sufficiently advanced technology can manipulate the "soul" as easily as we splice genes or mix chemicals in test tubes. If so, encounters with "extraterrestrials" may help provide a working knowledge of how to modify and transfer consciousness—abilities that seem remote to the current terrestrial state-of-the-art, but may prove invaluable

in a future where telepresence and virtual reality are integral to communication. Already, the capabilities of brain-machine interfaces are tantalizingly like the popular perception of telepathy, often thought of in strictly "paranormal" or even "magical" terms (Tonnies, 2009).

All of this brings us very close to—if not right into the very heart of—what is known as transhumanism. We're talking about us, as a species, becoming something amazing: a new type of human. We're talking about becoming *post*-human and, potentially, immortal. We're even talking about the merging of man and highly advanced technology in ways that, currently, boggle the mind.

Zoltan Istvan is the driving force behind the Transhumanist Party. It's a group based on the West Coast of the United States, and which has close to 10,000 members comprised of "largely rich Californians, technology geeks and scientists (sometimes all three)," as the UK's *Telegraph* newspaper noted (Bartlett, 2014). In 2016, Istvan ran for the office of President of the United States. History has shown that he did not achieve his goal. But that doesn't mean he won't achieve his other goal: immortality. He just might.

Istvan says that transhumanism "literally means *beyond human*. Transhumanists consist of life extensionists, techno-optimists, Singularitarians, biohackers, roboticists, AI [artificial intelligence] proponents, and futurists who embrace radical science and technology to improve the human condition. The most important aim for many transhumanists is to overcome human mortality, a goal some believe is achievable by 2045" (Istvan, 2014).

There are important and pressing questions that need to be asked when addressing Istvan's words. Namely, by radically altering the human species in an attempt to achieve never-ending life, will we still retain that which makes each and every one of us human? Or, will we become not just post-human, but *inhuman*? Maybe even *non*-human?

Nick Bostrom, a Swedish philosopher, author, and coeditor of a number of books, including *Human Enhancement* and *Superintelligence: Paths, Dangers, Strategies*, makes a good, relevant observation on this particularly thorny matter: "In Christian theology, some souls will be allowed by God to go to heaven after their time as corporal creatures is over. Before being admitted to heaven, the souls would undergo a purification process in which they would lose many of their previous bodily attributes" (Bostrom, 2003).

It's ironic, given the deep divides that very often come into play when the matter of science versus religion surfaces, that the effects transhumanism may have on us—namely, from the perspective of turning us into something radically different—are not at all far removed from the equally altered states that the purifying of the soul might also provoke.

Could Bostrom's words have a bearing on the seemingly completely emotionless nature of the Greys? Yes, they could. If, in the distant past, the Greys achieved immortality in a post-human (or, more correctly, a post-*alien*) situation, was it at the expense of their equivalent of our humanity? Perhaps, millennia ago, the Greys had their own version of the "three-score and ten" situation and had lives not too different from and not much longer than ours. Today, however, they are strange, emotion-free, machine-like entities. They live their eternal lives partly in the realm of the afterlife and partly in a 3D-based physical environment, and as the mood takes them or as circumstances dictate. And, it's all "thanks" to their immersion in the world of something very much akin to transhumanism. Immortality, then, may be achievable, but it just might come with a terrible, irreversible price. That price: the end of the human race as we understand it and the rise of something radically different.

An immortal human race may not be a bad thing, however. No doubt, there are those who believe it's feasible to live forever without compromising that which makes each and every one of us utterly unique.

"We Have to Work Out How This Bacteria Prevents Ageing"

In October 2015, a startling story surfaced that has a direct bearing on the attempts by us, the human race, to stay alive, *maybe forever*. It all revolved around a man named Anatoli Brouchkov of Moscow, Russia's State University. Rather incredibly, but also at potentially great risk to himself, since 2013 Brouchkov has been injecting himself with a particular strain of bacteria. It's not your everyday, common bacteria, however. Rather, it is an approximately three-and-a-half-million-years-old bacteria—Bacillus F—which was found in the harsh permafrost of Siberia, specifically on Mamontova Gora Mountain.

Incredibly, experiments on small animals—including mice and rats—and on both flora and human blood cells demonstrated that both fertility and life span were extended when injected with small amounts of the bacteria, and significantly so too. In some cases, the ancient bacteria also reversed damage to flora and increased the sperm count in elderly male mice. It was these discoveries and developments that led Brouchkov to become nothing less than his very own guinea pig. He was enthusiastic and not at all concerned by the controversial, dicey route he chose to take. He said that he had more energy, was seemingly immune to influenza, and was able to work for significantly longer periods of time. He admitted, however, that "it still needs more experiments. We have to work out how this bacteria prevents ageing. I think that is the way this science should develop. What is keeping that mechanism alive? And how can we use it for our own benefits?" (Horton, 2015).

Brouchkov's rationale for having no qualms about turning himself into a lab rat was that the people who lived in the region of the Mamontova Gora Mountain were (a) unaffected by lengthy exposure to the very same bacteria; and (b) noted for their lengthy life spans.

Doing the Best to Try and Live Longer

"It is nonsensical and counter-intuitive to believe that complex life was created only to end after a set period of time. An intelligent, complex being should be able to live indefinitely, or to put it in another way, it should not be allowed to die through ageing" ("Extreme Lifespans through Perpetual-equalizing Interventions (ELPIs)," 2016).

Those are the words of Marios Kyriazis, a medical doctor and someone who in 1992 established the British Longevity Society. Although Kyriazis believes that major breakthroughs in life extension are likely to be a reality one day, he doesn't believe it's on the immediate horizon. He admits that, right now, we are sorely limited to the far more conventional ways of trying to ensure we achieve long lives, such as eating healthily, engaging in exercise, not smoking cigarettes, and taking supplements. He is of the opinion that research in the fields of nanotechnology and stem cells may certainly have a bearing on how long, exactly, we might live for. Right now, though, he suggests we have to wait for that technology to reach such a level that it can have an appreciable and significant impact on us. At this particular moment in time, he stresses, we're not yet at that point. But, maybe, one day we will be.

Others disagree with Kyriazis, including those who believe that the answer to immortality will come via the splicing of human and machine: real-life equivalents of *Robocop* and *The Six Million Dollar Man*, and even the uploading of one's memories and life experiences into highly advanced computers. That process of uploading, of course, harks back to how the Raelians believe that the only way to have a continual existence is via the transfer of the human mind to another medium. One group prefers machines; the other believes that our destiny lies in the field of cloning.

"In Addition to Radical Life Extension, We're Going to Have Radical Life Expansion"

When it comes to the issue of the human race being radically altered in the future—perhaps even in the astonishingly near future—and possibly even becoming immortal, few can rival Ray Kurzweil in the controversy stakes. The director of engineering at Google, and a computer scientist, Kurzweil has made some jaw-dropping predictions for what may be in store by, perhaps, no later than 2045. It's his prediction that as computer technology develops at an exponential rate, and as nanotechnology becomes ever more advanced, we'll reach a tipping point that Kurzweil terms the Singularity.

That will be the moment when we become digitally immortal. Our minds will be uploaded into computers. We may even be able to live in both a physical and a digital state, jumping from one to the other as we see fit. And, while we are in our physical states, we will likely see our bodily organs increasingly replaced by sophisticated technology that will effectively transform us into cyborgs.

Although Kurzweil has been making such predictions for a long time, it was his presentation at the 2013, New York–based *Global Future 2045 International Congress* that really caught the attention of both the media and the public. It was a conference funded and organized by a Russian multimillionaire, Dmitry Itskov. Kurzweil's words were powerful and, for some, more than a bit daunting. He says that in all probability, as the years and the decades go by, we are very likely to become less biological in nature and to the point "where the non-biological part dominates and the biological part is not important any more. In fact the non-biological part—the machine part—will be so powerful it can completely model and understand the biological part. So even if that biological part went away, it wouldn't make any difference" (Woollaston, 2013).

Going down even more controversial paths, Kurzweil believes that as well as having physical bodies, and ones that are maybe more machine than human, we may also see the day when we have virtual lives—ones that will be able to operate in entirely virtual reality-based worlds and environments, and to the point where those virtual worlds will mirror the real world to a perfect degree. He stresses that we *do* need some form of physical body, and likely always will, because that is our natural state, but that as time passes it may become perfectly normal for us to be able to jump from a physical state to a virtual one and back again.

And, on the matter of the immortality that Kurzweil believes is getting ever closer, he offers a very important point that has a bearing on all of us, should our life spans and our lives head off into radical and new directions. He says, and with a great deal of justification, that it won't be enough for us to just have extended lives: we'll also need expansive lives. After all, what is the point of having immortality if one has nothing to do with all that extra, unending time?

What all of this tells us is that, barring some worldwide Armageddon-style event, in less than half a century we may well be living in a world in which no one ever dies. Even long-lived Methuselah himself—someone possibly genetically enhanced by the Anunnaki— would have been envious of what just might soon be on the cards for all of us.

Unveiling the Youth Pill

To demonstrate that such research is still progressing at a fast pace, Nancy Loyan Schuemann, in a June 8, 2016 article titled "A 'Fountain of Youth' Pill May Be Available Soon," wrote that a team of scientists had discovered that a "combination of 30 supplements, including Vitamins B, C and D, folic acid, cod liver oil, green tea extract, and more have reversed the effects of aging and prevent the loss of brain cells. Over the course of fifteen years, studies have been conducted on mice with amazing results on mice" (Schuemann, 2016).

In truly astonishing fashion, mice reaching the age of two—which is old for a mouse—began to, effectively, regain their youth. Arthritis declined, mental faculties increased to levels that one would expect to see in a much younger mouse, and even hunchbacks, a condition that mice can be affected by, lessened notably.

Schuemann also revealed that the studies undertaken on the mice led Professor Jennifer Lemon of the Hamilton, Ontario, Canada-based McMaster University, and a key person in the program, to say that the discoveries were profound and that they might very well have a large bearing on how we treat human disease in the future. Lemon, whose grandmother fell victim to dementia and died at 84, says that this particular breakthrough offers a great deal of promise for people who are suffering from neurological-based conditions. There are solid reasons for thinking this will certainly be the case: despite us being acutely different animals, there is very little difference between the way we are affected by neurological diseases and how mice are affected by them. What works for the mice may soon work for us, too.

All being well, trials on people will begin as early as 2018, and will hopefully have significant, positive bearing upon such conditions as Lou Gehrig's disease, Parkinson's, and Alzheimer's.

CONCLUSIONS

Unlike the lives of the mysterious entities that fill the pages of this book, our story is not never-ending. That's to say, it's now time to make some final observations on the matter of aliens both ancient and modern, and to answer one important question: what, exactly, can we say about this curious phenomenon of extraterrestrial immortality? Let's take a look at this complex matter. The question may be a single one, but it has numerous strands attached to it.

First and foremost, it is very important to note that regardless of where one personally stands on the matter of long-lived aliens, gods, demigods, and even a small elite band of humans, no one can deny that such accounts proliferate and have done so for thousands of years, and on a worldwide basis, no less. As we have also seen, those accounts are by no means restricted to the distant past. The matter of immortality in the modern era—and in relation to the alien abduction controversy—is very much an ongoing issue, and an issue that clearly has a bearing upon national security and official secrecy, too. But let us not get ahead of ourselves. Let's break things down and see what conclusions we can reach.

A case can be made that there are two distinct types of immortality: (a) one that has been achieved via highly advanced technology, science, cloning, and medicine; and (b) one that is entirely natural, but which to this day is still steeped in mystery, namely, that which revolves around the soul or the life-force of, just perhaps, all living creatures on the planet.

To what extent the Anunnaki believed in the existence of an immortal soul is, in many respects, moot. It's also almost irrelevant. After all, why worry about an immortal life as a soul-based, supernatural entity when one can have an unending physical, three-dimensional life? The very same could be said of the gods—or the extraterrestrials—of ancient Egypt, Greece, and India, too. In all likelihood, physical life was, and still is, as valuable to them as it is to us. And finding a way to keep that life from becoming extinguished would have been paramount for the Anunnaki, as well as for any other early aliens that may have visited the Earth thousands of years ago.

As for the human component of all this, it's hardly surprising that the short-lived, envious people of the era in which the Anunnaki dominated the planet came to view this mighty, space-race as gods. After all, they soared across the skies in incredible machines, they performed amazing feats of engineering, and—undoubtedly, the most important and relevant portion of the story—whereas the human population aged and died, the Anunnaki did precisely neither. They were, for all intents and purposes, eternal. In light of all this, one can make a very good case that it was practically inevitable that the Anunnaki would be perceived as paranormal deities. The Anunnaki may even have actively and widely encouraged such a belief, primarily to try and ensure a culture of obedience, subservience, and fear on the part of the human race—a race that the Anunnaki created, manipulated, and used as a slave-based commodity. There is, however, another human component to all of this.

As we have seen, it wasn't just the all-powerful entities from Nibiru who were blessed with massive life spans; it was also a certain, select band of people. Their names, as we have seen, included the likes of

Methuselah, Seth, Adam, Kenan, and Mahalalel. In our terms, many of this specific band of elite reached close to 1,000 years of age, before finally expiring. There were, too, those who sought out immortality, but failed in their quests—the most famous example being that of King Gilgamesh, the demigod who wanted much more, but who didn't quite get it. All of this tells us that humans were not born near-immortal and still aren't. But there *were* ways in which the natural process of human aging could be prevented or, at the very least, slowed down to an incredible degree, and all thanks to the direct intervention of the Anunnaki.

This affair of a long, interconnected family that began with Adam (or, rather, with the Adama) and which extended to Jesus, demonstrates something incredible: *not a single one of us, potentially, is limited to the biblical three score and ten.* We are not limited to 80, 90, or even a century. Survival is solely down to science—science that the Anunnaki shared with certain humans and for no other reason than it served a purpose in relation to their long-term agenda on Earth. But, unfortunately for us today, it is science that has been lost, deliberately buried, or forgotten. Unless, that is, we one day stumble upon it or the extraterrestrial gods return and share it with us, as they did to a degree in biblical times.

In terms of how, exactly, immortality and life spans of amazing lengths were achieved, we see a certain trend that runs through just about each and every one of the old legends: it had nothing to do with the supernatural wave of a hand from an equally supernatural being. Instead, it had everything to do with the ingestion of certain substances that didn't just slow down the ticking clock of life, but which brought the hands of the clock to a complete halt.

The skeptics would, of course, state that tales of the likes of White Powder Gold, Amrita, the Fountain of Youth, Manna, and the secrets of alchemy were directly born out of nothing stranger than mythology, legend, and folklore. But what if that's not the case? What if, from the gold-obsessed Anunnaki of hundreds of thousands of years ago to the ancient Egyptians and the Greeks, these eerie elixirs were all too real? Their existences, and their abilities to give a decisive middle finger to death, would explain a great deal about how and why certain ancient humans had such extensive lives, how and why the same was the case for the "gods," and also how and why, for us today, we're unfortunately out of the loop. Or are we? Maybe we're not. At least, that may be the case for some of us.

This latter point brings us to the matter of conspiracies, cover-ups, and classified programs designed to seek out the secrets of the past. On this matter, a persuasive case can be made to the effect that some-one, at least, within the U.S. Government, intelligence community, or the military (perhaps a combination of all three) has spent a great deal of time, money, and manpower to try and unravel the mysteries of the past, as a means to dictate the future, and also to dictate how long we live. Or, how long a certain, select elite may live. The looting of the Museum of Baghdad, the stories suggesting that top-secret research into the field of immortality has been undertaken at the Utah-based Dugway Proving Ground, the matter of the connections between the invasion of Iraq in 2003 and the saga of Gilgamesh, and the words of Michael Salla and Jim Marrs collectively make an intriguing case for something startling: the matter of immortality is taken very seriously at a governmental and highly secret level.

The angle of government interest in life evermore is not without its disturbing aspects, however. As we've seen, more than two decades ago the controversial Bob Lazar claimed to have read a stash of clas-sified documents—at a portion of Nevada's Area 51 called S-4—that claimed the human race was not just a genetically altered race, but a race of what our extraterrestrial creators termed containers. Lazar suggested or, perhaps, hinted that we might be containers of souls, souls that the aliens had a deep interest in. What that interest might be, we don't know. What we do know, however, is that Whitley Strieber of *Communion* fame has gone on record as stating that the so-called Grey type of alien has one, primary agenda: the recycling of human souls. The data provided to Strieber, by what he terms the Visitors, suggests that immortality is inevitable for us, albeit in the sense that we're constantly being placed into new bodies and new identities as one body dies and another is born.

On a slightly similar path, we've seen the theories of Nigel Kerner who suggests that, yes, the Greys do have an interest in the human soul, but it's a downright nefarious interest; one which has at its heart a program designed to provide the Greys with the one thing they lack: an immortal soul. If matters relative to both human and alien immortality are known to a secret faction within the government, then the scenarios described by both Strieber and Kerner would undoubtedly be of concern to those who wish to see order, civilization, and society kept in check—rather than in a constant state of combined terror, anarchy, and disorder, if the truth of how our immortal souls are being used and manipulated became widespread, public knowledge. In that sense, the issue of immortality and all of its implications may amount to a dangerous and deadly game of chess. And we're the unknowing pawns.

Moving on, there's the matter of how, one day, we may finally perfect the kinds of science and medicine that were second nature to the Anunnaki, hundreds of thousands of years ago. If we do conquer death—whether alone or with the help of extraterrestrials—will we come to view ourselves as more than human or, perhaps, as far less than human? Maybe we'll have a mindset so radically altered by our ability to no longer die that we will think of our species as gods, just as the ancients did when it came to the Anunnaki and their presence on our planet.

This latter issue of how immortality might change us—maybe the way it changed things for the Anunnaki in the past and how it continues to mold the Greys today—brings up some interesting issues. For example, just because we might one day be able to state that yes, finally, we have conquered death, does that mean we *should* conquer it? That may sound like a strange question. After all, each and every one of us wants to avoid death, right? Right! So far, that has not happened—to the best of our knowledge. But if such an announcement was made tomorrow, that by drinking a certain cocktail on a daily basis we could never age and never die, how would our lives change?

Part of what makes us what and who we are is the knowledge and awareness that we are all on time limits. And they are not particularly long ones, either. That's why we try and live life to its absolute fullest. It's a case of grabbing it while you have it *because, one day, you won't*. If, however, we are all placed in a state where death becomes completely meaningless to us and there's no need to do much of anything because we really *do* have all the time in the world, will we, after a few centuries of constant "been here, done that," be reduced to bored and almost morose entities with no goals, no sense of urgency and excitement, and, ironically, nothing to live for, except for life itself?

There's a more disturbing scenario, too. Although, as we have seen, the Anunnaki may have been immortals, they could still die. And they knew it all too well. For the Anunnaki, the aging process may have stopped, but their bodies were not protected from the devastating effects of nuclear war, violent, physical trauma, and the kinds of destruction that occurred when faction turned on faction during the period that led to the annihilation of the people of Sumer, Sodom, and Gomorrah.

Keeping that in mind, if we are destined to no longer age, but (just like the Anunnaki) we realize that we could still die in a violent car accident, in an aircraft crash, or via a terrorist's bomb, would we all be reduced to staying at home, forever peeking through the curtains and worrying about what might await us outside? Will we be fearful of doing just about anything that might take away life, our now-endless commodity? Undoubtedly, when you have immortality you want to hang on to it. In light of that, we may find ourselves reduced to a collective situation where the best way to hang on to immortality is to stay indoors and do nothing—forever.

Then there's the matter of who, exactly, will benefit from immortality? Will it be all of us? Or will it be a global elite and no one else? If it is the latter scenario, then the former are hardly likely to sit back and accept they will have 80 or so years, while that same elite gets infinity. Global chaos surely won't be far behind as billions mount an uprising against the several million elite. If, however, everyone is granted immortality, does that mean no more children? After all, there is only so much space on our tiny planet. Could we live in a world, forever, where children no longer exist, specifically because with no one dying there's no more room for anyone else? Would we even want to live like that? How would we cope in situations where family units of mom, dad, and the kids are nothing but memories?

Perhaps such questions taxed the minds of aliens thousands and even millions of years ago. Maybe, with immortality there comes a kind of almost inevitable, soulless, dull, and detached existence. One gets a life that doesn't end, but the price in terms of one's humanity is tragically high. Quite possibly that's what happened to the Greys, who are typically described as being largely emotionless and unable to bond, but who may not have always been like that. Perhaps, today, they have no memories of who or what they once were.

Before we all get overexcited by the prospect of never ending up in an urn over the fireplace, or six feet under the ground, we should take note of the above and keep in mind the following words of the Immortality Institute. They say something notable that harks back to the days of the ancient gods that instilled both fear and reverence in early humans:

> The Cumaean Sybil, adored by Apollo, is granted a thousand
> years of life, but because she spurns the love of the god, he

withholds eternal youth and she suffers on and on. Tithonus, beloved of Eos, the Goddess of Dawn, is granted immortality but forgets to ask for eternal youth, so he ages forever in what Tennyson has him call "cruel immortality." Prometheus is by nature an immortal, but for having stolen fire for humanity, his immortality becomes an eternity of suffering (Immortality Institute, 2004).

The Immortality Institute goes on to note that everlasting life may be "a fine thing in its proper place, but ironic, indeed tragic, when corrupted" (ibid.).

We, as a species, would do very well to heed those words should, one day, immortality be in our grasp, just like it once was for our ancient gods from the stars. Perhaps living for the moment is better than living forever.

BIBLIOGRAPHY

"10th Planet Discovered." http://science.nasa.gov/science-news/science
-at-nasa/2005/29jul_planetx/. July 29, 2005.

"About Methuselah." https://mfoundation.org/about. 2016.

"Aetos Deus." http://www.theoi.com/Ther/AetosDios.html. 2016.

"Albinism." https://medlineplus.gov/ency/article/001479.htm. August 23,
2016.

Alford, Alan. *Gods of the New Millennium*. Southampton, UK: Eridu Books,
1996.

Alouf, Michel M. *History of Baalbek*. San Diego, CA: Book Tree, 1999.

Allingham, William. "The Fairies." http://www.sff.net/people/doyle
macdonald/l_fairie.htm. 2015.

"Ambrosia." http://www.greekmythology.com/Myths/Elements/Ambrosia
/ambrosia.html. 2016.

"Ambrosia—Food of the Greek Gods." http://www.loggia.com/myth
/ambrosia.html. 2016.

"Amrita-Ambrosia: The nectar of immortality."
https://yogakinisis.wordpress.com/2013/05/14/amrita-ambrosia-the
-nectar-of-immortality/. May 14, 2013.

"Ancient Chinese Alchemists and their Search for Immortality." http://
www.monkeytree.org/silkroad/gunpowder/china1.html. 2016.

"Ancient Flying Machines." http://www.thelivingmoon.com/47brother
thebig/03files/Vimanas_Mercury_Vortex_ Technology.html. 2008.

"Anunnaki." http://www.halexandria.org/dward185.htm. February 5,
2009.

Appel, Daniel. "5 Ancient Legends about the Secret of Immortality." http://ultraculture.org/blog/2014/05/05/5-ancient-legends -secret-immortality/. May 25, 2014.

Ashliman, D.L. "The Creation of Life on Earth According to the Raelian Movement." http://www.pitt.edu/~dash/rael.html. January 8, 2003.

"Baalbek." http://ancientaliensdebunked.com/references-and-transcripts /baalbek/. 2015.

Ballard, Guy. Letter to Stanley Carter, March 18, 1931.

Bartlett, Jamie. "Meet the Transhumanist Party: 'Want to live forever? Vote for me.'" http://www.telegraph.co.uk/technology/11310031 /Meet-the-Transhumanist-Party-Want-to-live-forever-Vote-for-me .html. December 23, 2014.

Bartlett, Zane. "The Hayflick Limit." https://embryo.asu.edu/pages /hayflick-limit. November 14, 2014.

Benedict, Tim. "The First Global Nuclear War And a Cover-up of HISTORICAL Proportions!" http://ancientnuclearwar.com/. 2015.

Bingham, John. "Average life expectancy heading for 100." http://www .telegraph.co.uk/news/politics/11348561/Average-life-expectancy -heading-for-100.html. January 15, 2015.

Birnes, William J. *The Everything UFO Book*. Avon, MA: Adams Media, 2012.

Bishop, Greg. "Frank Stranges Passes Away." http://www.ufomystic.com /wake-up-down-there/frank-stranges-passes/. November 21, 2008.

Bishop, Kitty. *The Tao of Mermaids*. Bloomington, IN: Balboa Press, 2010.

Blum, Ralph, and Judy Blum. *Beyond Earth*. New York: Bantam Books, 1978.

Bostrom, Nick. "Human Genetic Enhancements: A Transhumanist Perspective." *Journal of Value Inquiry* 37(4): 493-506. http://www .nickbostrom.com/ethics/genetic.html. 2003.

Boyd, Jade. "'Quadrapeutics' works in preclinical study of hard-to-treat tumors." http://news.rice.edu/2014/06/01/quadrapeutics-works-in -preclinical-study-of-hard-to-treat-tumors-2/#sthash.vmQV5X8T .dpuf. June 1, 2014.

"Brother Rael." http://www.bibliotecapleyades.net/bb/rael.htm. 2016.

Brown, Tom. "Battle Lines." http://blog.seattletimes.nwsource.com/iraq /tombrown/archives/000823.html. April 17, 2003.

Buck, William. *Mahabharata*. New York: Meridian, 1987.

Burkeman, Oliver. "Bush's cultural aides quit over sack of Baghdad's treasures." https://www.theguardian.com/world/2003/apr/18 /internationaleducationnews.education. April 18, 2003.

Bush, President George. Speech, March 19, 2003.

Butler, Hiram. *The Goal of Life*. Applegate, CA: Esoteric Publishing Company, 1908.

Caron, Matt. "Amrita: Nectar of the Gods." http://blog.sivanaspirit.com /amrita-nectar-gods/. 2016.

"Cauldron-born." https://sff.net/people/hsfayle/cauldron.htm. 2016.

"Changelings and Fairy Babies." https://myndandmist.wordpress. com/2012/06/24/changelings-and-fairy-babies/. June 24, 2012.

Charles, R.H. *The Book of Enoch*. Oxford, UK: Oxford University Press, 1912.

Childress, David Hatcher. "Hollow Earth, Vimana Aircraft of Ancient India & Atlantis." http://davidhatcherchildress.com/hollow-earth -vimana-aircraft-ancient-india-atlantis. 2016.

——. *Technology of the Gods: The Incredible Sciences of the Ancients*. Kempton, IL: Adventures Unlimited Press, 2015.

——. *The Anti-Gravity Book*. Kempton, IL: Adventures Unlimited Press, 2003.

——. *Vimana Aircraft of Ancient India & Atlantis*. Kempton, IL: Adventures Unlimited, 1988.

Clark, Gerald R. *The Anunnaki of Nibiru*. CreateSpace Independent Publishing Platform, 2013.

Clarke, David, and Andy Roberts. *Flying Saucerers*. Loughborough, UK: Alternative Albion, 2007.

"Cloning." https://www.genome.gov/25020028/cloning-fact-sheet/. May 11, 2016.

"Comte Saint-Germain." http://www.alchemylab.com/count_saint _germain.htm. 2016.

Conroy, Ed. *Report on Communion*. New York: Avon Books, 1989.

"Conversations: Building Trust in Iraq." http://archive.archaeology.org /0401/etc/conversations.html. 2004.

Coppens, Philip. "The Rise of the Watchers." http://philipcoppens.com /watchers.html. 2016.

Corso, Philip J., with William J. Birnes. *The Day After Roswell*. New York: Simon & Schuster, 1997.

"Count St. Germain—Alchemist." http://www.crystalinks.com/stgermain .html. 2016.

Crawford, Peter. "Alien Abduction." http://ufomysteryandmeaning. blogspot.com/2011/09/alien-abduction.html. 2012.

Cutchin, Joshua. *A Trojan Feast*. San Antonio, TX: Anomalist Books, 2015.

D'Arc, Joan. "Are Zecharia Sitchin and Vatican Official Monsignor
　　Balducci Really Climbing the Same Path to Ascension?" http://
　　www.bibliotecapleyades.net/sitchin/esp_sitchin_4.htm. October
　　20, 2000.

Dakks, Brian. "Eve: First Human Clone?" http://cbsnews.com.news/eve
　　-first-human-clone/. December 28, 2002.

De Lafayette, Maximillien. *The New De Lafayette Mega Encyclopedia of
　　Anunnaki. Volume 5.* Lulu, 2010.

Demontis, Alessandro. "Ningishzidda and Ishkur." http://www
　　.bibliotecapleyades.net/thot/esp_thot_11.htm. December 2009.

Deschamps, Justin. "Bob Lazar | Secret Space Program Whistleblower
　　from the 1990's: Element 115, ET History of the Human Race, Dr.
　　Michael Salla Analysis." http://sitsshow.blogspot.com/2016/04
　　/Bob-Lazar-Secret-Space-Program-Whistleblower-from-the-1990s
　　-Element-115-ET-History-of-the-Human-Race-Dr-Michael-Salla
　　-Analysis.html. April 2, 2016.

Diaz, Frank. *The Gospel of the Toltecs: The Life and Teachings of Quetzalcoatl.*
　　Rochester, VT: Bear & Co., 2002.

Drake, W.R. *Alien Space Gods of Ancient Greece and Rome.* New Brunswick,
　　NJ: Global Communications, 2011.

Editors of Encyclopedia Britannica. "Quetzalcoatl." http://www.britannica
　　.com/EBchecked/topic/487168/Quetzalcoatl. August 26, 2014.

"Elohim Meaning." http://www.abarim-publications.com/Meaning
　　/Elohim.html#.V4aJK6Lympo. 2016.

"Enki and Ninhursag." http://www.gatewaystobabylon.com/myths/texts
　　/retellings/enkininhur.htm. 2015.

"Epic of Gilgamesh—Sumerian Flood Story 2750-2500 BCE." http://www
　　.historywiz.com/primarysources/sumerianflood.html. 2015.

"The Epic of Gilgamesh." http://www.sparknotes.com/lit/gilgamesh
　　/section9.rhtml. 2015.

The Epic of Gilgamesh. Translated by Andrew George. London, UK: Penguin
　　Classics, 2003.

"Exodus 16." http://biblehub.com/niv/exodus/16.htm. 2016.

"Exodus 32." http://biblehub.com/niv/exodus/32.htm. 2016.

"Extreme Lifespans through Perpetual-equalising Interventions (ELPIs)."
　　http://www.elpistheory.info/. 2016.

"Faerie Folklore in Medieval Tales an Introduction." http://www.
　　academia.edu/300335/Faerie_Folklore_in_Medieval_Tales_an
　　_Introduction. 2015.

Farley, Peter R. "The Anunnaki Branch Grows." http://www.bibliotec apleyades.net/sociopolitica/the_experiment/experiment12.htm . 2016.

"First Human Clone Born, Cult Chemist Claims." http://foxnews.com /story/2002/12/27/first-human-clone-born-cult-chemist-claims .html. December 27, 2002.

Fowler, Raymond E. *The Andreasson Affair.* Englewood Cliffs, N.J.: Prentice-Hall, 1979.

———. *The Andreasson Legacy.* New York: Marlowe & Co., 1997.

Frazer, Sir James George. *The Golden Bough.* London, UK: 1890.

Freer, Neil. "Sapiens Rising: Beyond the Babel Factor." http://anunnakis .com/category/neil-freer/. March 19, 2012.

Friedman, Stanton T., and Kathleen Marden. *Captured! The Betty and Barney Hill UFO Experience.* Pompton Plains, NJ: New Page Books, 2007.

Fuller, John G. *The Interrupted Journey.* New York: The Dial Press, 1965.

Gardner, Laurence. *Genesis of the Grail Kings.* New York: Bantam Press, 1999.

———. "Lost Secrets of the Sacred Ark." http://www.graal.co.uk/lost secretslecture.php. 2016.

Gary. "From Cauldron to Grail in Celtic Mythology." http://celticmythpodshow.com/blog/from-cauldron-to-grail-in-celtic -mytholgy/. March 3, 2013.

"Genesis 5." http://biblehub.com/niv/genesis/5.htm. 2016.

"Gilgamesh tomb believed found." http://news.bbc.co.uk/2/hi/science /nature/2982891.stm. April 29, 2003.

"Godsend: The Movie, Clonaid: The Reality." http://www.clonaid.com /news.php?item.15.1. 2009.

Gollner, Adam Leith. *Immortality.* New York: Scribner, 2013.

Good, Timothy. *Alien Liaison.* London, UK: Arrow Books Limited, 1992.

"The Great Flood: the Epic of Atrahatis." http://www.livius.org/fa-fn /flood/flood3-t-atrahasis.html. 2015.

"Great Gods of the Celts: Manannan mac Lir." http://manannan.net /library/comparative.html. 2015.

"Group claims human cloning success." https://www.theguardian.com /science/2002/dec/27/genetics.science. December 27, 2002.

Hall, Manly P. *The Secret Teachings of All Ages.* Mineola, NY: Dover Publications, 2010.

Hanks, Micah. "Comte de St. Germain: Rosicrucian, Ascended Master, or Immortal." http://mysteriousuniverse.org/2013/11

/comte-de-saint-germain-rosicrucian-ascended-master-or
-immortal/. November 27, 2013.

Hardy, Chris H. *DNA of the Gods: The Anunnaki Creation of Eve and the Alien Battle for Humanity*. Rochester, VT: Bear & Company, 2014.

———. *Wars of the Anunnaki: Nuclear Self-Destruction in Ancient Sumer*. Rochester, VT: Bear & Company, 2016.

Hayes, Anna. "Anna Hayes on Mono Atomic Gold." http://educate
-yourself.org/cn/annahayesmonoatomicgold2000.shtml. 2000.

Heiberg, Jeanne. "Manna: God's Boundless Generosity." http://www
.catechist.com/articles_view.php?article_id=2348. 2016.

"History." http://www.clonaid.com/page.php?7. 2009.

Hopkins, Budd. *Intruders: The Incredible Visitations at Copley Woods*. New York: Random House, 1987.

———. *Missing Time*. New York: Ballantine Books, 1981.

Horn, Thomas R. "They Part 3." http://www.newswithviews.com/Horn
/thomas165.htm. July 24, 2011.

Horner, I.B. "The Blessed One's City of Dhamma." http://www.access toinsight.org/lib/authors/horner/bl130.html. 2016.

Horton, Helena. "Russian scientist says he is stronger and healthier after injecting himself with 'eternal life' bacteria." http://www.telegraph .co.uk/news/health/11901105/Russian-scientist-says-he-is
-stronger-and-healthier-after-injecting-himself-with-eternal-life
-bacteria.html. September 30, 2015.

"Human Cloning Laws." http://www.ncsl.org/research/human-cloning
-laws.aspx. 2016.

Immortality Institute. *The Scientific Conquest of Death*. Libros en Red, 2004.

"In vitro fertilization (IVF)." http://www.mayoclinic.org/tests-procedures
/in-vitro-fertilization/home/ovc-20206838. 2016.

"Introducing Gilgamesh." http://www.bcconline.com/huma5/gilgamesh
.htm. 2015.

Isaacson, Betsy. "Silicon Valley is Trying to Make Humans Immortal—and Finding Some Success." http://www.newsweek.com/2015/03/13
/silicon-valley-trying-make-humans-immortal-and-finding-some
-success-311402.html. March 25, 2015

Istvan, Zoltan. "A New Generation of Transhumanists is Emerging." http://www.huffingtonpost.com/zoltan-istvan/a-new-generation
-of-trans_b_4921319.html. May 10, 2014.

Jarayam, V. "The Story of Sagara Manthan." http://www.hinduwebsite
.com/churning.asp. April 16, 2016.

"John 6:51." http://biblehub.com/john/6-51.htm. 2015.

Jones, Mary. "Manannan mac Lir." http://www.maryjones.us/jce
/manannan.html. 2003.

Kasten, Len. "Is There a Disturbing Hidden Agenda in Global Events?"
Atlantis Rising 41, September/October 2003.

Kerner, Nigel. *Grey Aliens and the Harvesting of Souls.* Rochester, VT: Bear &
Company, 2010.

———. *Song of the Greys.* London, UK: Hodder and Stoughton, 1997.

———. "Visions of the Future—Sim Card Man." *New Dawn Magazine* 119,
March/April 2010. http://www.newdawnmagazine.com/articles
/visions-of-the-future-sim-card-man.

King, Godfre Ray. *Unveiled Mysteries.* Chicago, IL: St. Germain Press, 1934.

Knight, Kevin. "Manna." http://www.newadvent.org/cathen/09604a
.htm. 2012.

Knight-Jadczyk, Laura. "Alien Abduction, Demonic Possession, and The
Legend of The Vampire." http://www.cassiopaea.org/cass/demons
.htm. 2016.

Lady Gregory. *Gods and Fighting Men.* London, UK: John Murray, 1905.

Lamont, Tom. "I'll do the first human head transplant." https://www
.theguardian.com/science/2015/oct/03/will-first-human-head
-transplant-happen-in-2017. October 3, 2015.

Lauria, Joe. "Clonaid's Secret Attempt to Clone Human Being in West
Virginia Revealed." *Times*, August 12, 2001. http://www.rense.com
/general12/west.htm.

Lawler, Andrew. "Impending War Stokes Battle Over Fate of Iraqi
Antiquities." http://science.sciencemag.org/content/299/5607
/news-summaries. January 31, 2003.

———. "National Museum Baghdad: 10 Years Later." http://www
.archaeology.org/exclusives/articles/779-national-museum
-baghdad-looting-iraq. 2016.

Lessin, Sasha Alex. "Our Secret Government's Amid War Between Nibiru
King Nannar and Prince Marduk." http://enkispeaks.com/2015
/06/our-secret-governments-amid-war-between-anunnaki-princes
-marduk-nannar-by-sasha-alex-lessin-ph-d/. June 20, 2015.

Lindemann, Michael. *UFOs and the Alien Presence.* Blue Water Publishing,
1995.

Lombardi, Michael. "Communion—A Review." http://oceanopportunity.
com/communion-review/. September 26, 2011.

Longnecker, Dwight. "Why Did God Destroy Sodom and Gomorrah?"
http://www.patheos.com/blogs/standingonmyhead/2015/06/why
-did-god-destroy-sodom-and-gomorrah.html. June 25, 2015.

Mack, John E. *Abduction*. New York: Ballantine Books, 1995.

————. *Passport to the Cosmos*. New York: Three Rivers Press, 1999.

"Manannan mac Lir (and some Norse Connections)." https://earthand starryheaven.com/2015/05/19/mannan-mac-lir/. May 19, 2015.

Marchand, Peter. "The Churning of the Ocean." http://www.sanatan society.org/indian_epics_and_stories/the_churning_of_the _ocean .htm#.V4Uo76Lympo. 2016.

Marden, Kathleen, and Denise Stoner. *The Alien Abduction Files*. Wayne, NJ: New Page Books, 2013.

Markey, Sean. "First Invisibility Cloak Tested Successfully, Scientists Say." http://news.nationalgeographic.com/news/2006/10/061019 -invisible-cloak.html. October 19, 2006.

Marrs, Jim. "Future Technology from the Past." http://jimmarrs.com /news_events/news/future-technology-from-the-past-2/. September 17, 2004.

————. *Our Occulted History*. New York: Harper-Collins Publishers, 2013.

————. *The Terror Conspiracy*. New York: Disinformation Books, 2006.

————. *The Terror Conspiracy Revisited*. New York: Disinformation Books, 2011.

Maxwell, Jordan. "Jordan Maxwell Interviews Zecharia Sitchin." http:// www.bibliotecapleyades.net/sitchin/esp_sitchin_19.htm. 1997.

McDowell, Natasha. "Dutch clone claimed—but no proof." https://www .newscientist.com/article/dn3230-dutch-clone-claimed-but-no -proof/. January 6, 2003.

Melton, John Gordon. "I AM movement." https://www.britannica.com /topic/I-AM-movement. 2016.

Menger, Howard. *From Outer Space To You*. Clarksburg, WV: Saucerian Books, 1959.

"The Message." http://www.rael.org/message. 2016.

Mills, Ted. "20 New Lines from the Epic of Gilgamesh Discovered in Iraq, Adding New Details to the Story." http://www.openculture .com/2015/10/20-new-lines-from-the-epic-of-gilgamesh -discovered-in-iraq-adding-new-dimensions-to-the-story.html. October 25, 2015.

Mitchell, Stephen. *Gilgamesh: A New English Version*. New York: Atria Books, 2006.

"Monatomic Gold." http://www.femalefirst.co.uk/board/viewtopic.php?t =78920. June 20, 2006.

"The Myth of Manannan Mac Lir." http://www.isleofman.com/welcome /mythology-and-folklore/manannan-mac-lir/. 2015.

Nagasena, Ven. *The Questions of King Milinda.* CreateSpace, 2015.

"News." http://www.clonaid.com/page.php?18. 2009.

"The Nippur Expedition." https://oi.uchicago.edu/research/projects/nippur-expedition. 2014.

O'Connell, Tony. "Zechariah Sitchin." http://atlantipedia.ie/samples/tag/zecharia-sitchin/. December 16, 2012.

"The Olympian Gods." http://www.greek-gods.org/olympian-gods.php. 2016.

"ORMUS: The Elixir of Life." http://www.ormusmanna.com/ormus-the-elixir-of-life/. 2016.

Orozko, Chela. "The Legend of Quetzalcoatl." http://www.inside-mexico.com/the-legend-of-quetzalcoatl-by-chela-orozco/. September 30, 2013.

Osborn, David K. "Achilles and his Vulnerable Heel." http://www.greekmedicine.net/mythology/achilles.html. 2015.

Parsons, John J. "Hebrew Names of God." http://www.hebrew4christians.com/Names_of_G-d/Elohim/elohim.html. 2016.

Pattanaik, Devdutt. "Good deva-bad asura divide misleading." *Times of India,* http://timesofindia.indiatimes.com/india/Good-deva-bad-asura-divide-misleading/articleshow/51162479.cms.

Poole, Robert M. "Looting Iraq." http://www.smithsonianmag.com/making-a-difference/looting-iraq-16813540/?no-ist. February 2008.

Pratt, David. "The Count of Saint-Germain." http://davidpratt.info/st-germain2.htm. September 2012.

"Precious Metals in Medicine—How Gold Can Treat Cancer." http://orogoldschool.com/news/precious-metals-in-medicine-how-gold-can-treat-cancer/. 2016.

"Psalm 90." http://biblehub.com/kjv/psalms/90.htm. 2012.

Pye, Lloyd. *Everything You Know is Wrong.* Madeira Beach, FL: Adamu Press, 1997.

———. "What is Intervention Theory?" http://www.lloydpye.com/intervention/Intro-WhatIsIntervention.htm. 2011.

Pynes, Christopher A. "Human Cloning: Legal Aspects." http://www.els.net/WileyCDA/ElsArticle/refId-a0005200.html. December 2009.

Quora. "Which land of modern world is the Patal-Lok the place under the sea, as it was mentioned in Old Hindu manuscripts and stories?" https://www.quora.com/Which-land-of-modern-world-is-the-Patal-Lok-the-place-under-the-sea-as-it-was-mentioned-in-Old-Hindu-manuscripts-and-stories#!n=12. August 23, 2013.

"Rael: Singer/Songwriter." http://www.rael.org/rael/?singer. 2016.

Rawlinson, Sir Henry Creswicke, and John Gardner Wilkinson. *History of Herodotus.* New York: Scribner, Welford and Armstrong, 1875.

Redfern, Nick. *Bloodline of the Gods.* Wayne, NJ: New Page Books, 2015.

———. *Keep Out!* Wayne, NJ: New Page Books, 2012.

———. "Nigel Kerner & Soul-Harvesting." http://eventsfinal.blogspot.com/2010/09/nigel-kerner-soul-harvesting.html. September 27, 2010.

———. "Valiant Thor: A New Sighting?" Unpublished article, 2015.

———. *The Pyramids and the Pentagon.* Wayne, NJ: New Page Books, 2012.

———. *Weapons of the Gods.* Wayne, NJ: New Page Books, 2016.

Ritter, Malcolm. "Company claims birth of human clone; experts are skeptical." http://journaltimes.com/news/national/company-claims-birth-of-human-clone-experts-are-skeptical/article_ff5f2e99-11f3-5e85-b2d4-db74cf8e49ac.html. December 28, 2002.

Rose, Damon. "The people who think Noah had albinism." http://www.bbc.com/news/blogs-ouch-26870465. April 3, 2014.

Rudd, Steve. "The Epic of Gilgamesh." http://www.noahs-ark.tv/noahs-ark-flood-creation-stories-myths-epic-of-gilgamesh-neo-babylonian-akkadian-cuneiform-ut-napistim-tablet11-1150bc.htm. 2015.

Sabrina. "Cymidei Cymeinfoll." http://www.goddessaday.com/western-european/cymidei-cymeinfoll. June 9, 2008.

Salla, Michael E. "An Exopolitical Perspective on the Preemptive War against Iraq." http://exopolitics.org/Study-Paper2.htm. February 3, 2003.

Schuemann, Nancy Loyan. "A 'Fountain of Youth' Pill May be Available Soon." http://mysteriousuniverse.org/2016/06/a-fountain-of-youth-pill-may-be-available-soon/. June 8, 2016.

Sitchin, Zecharia. *Divine Encounters.* New York: Avon Books, 1995.

———. *Genesis Revisited.* New York: Avon Books, 1990.

———. "In the News—Baalbek. War Comes to the 'Landing Place.'" http://www.sitchin.com/landplace.htm. 2006.

———. "The Case of the Evil Wind: Climate Study Corroborates Sumer's Nuclear Fate." http://www.sitchin.com/evilwind.htm. November 2001.

———. *The Cosmic Code.* New York: Avon Books, 1998.

———. *The Lost Realms.* New York: Avon Books, 1990.

———. *The 12th Planet.* New York: Harper-Collins, 2007.

———. *The Wars of Gods and Men.* New York: Harper-Collins, 2007.

————. *There Were Giants Upon the Earth*. Rochester, VT: Bear & Co., 2010.

————. *When Time Began*. New York: Avon Books, 1993.

"Small Greys." http://thehybridsproject.objectreport.com/p/small-Greys .html. 2015.

Sokolov, Michael. "Michael Sokolov Briefing Paper." http://www .exopoliticssouthafrica.org/download/Michael_Sokolov_Briefing _Paper.pdf. 2016.

Steiger, Brad. *Real Zombies*. Canton, MI: Visible Ink Press, 2010.

Strange World. "It's a Strange World." http://www.itsastrangeworld.com /aliens-working-u-s-government/. April 12, 2014.

Stranges, Frank. Lecture at the Edgar Cayce Foundation, 1968.

————. *Stranger at the Pentagon*. New Brunswick, NJ: Inner Light Publications, 1991.

Strieber, Whitley. *Communion*. New York: William Morrow & Co., 1987.

————. "Temple of Ishtar Discovered." http://www.unknowncountry .com/news/temple-ishtar-discovered. October 23, 2001.

————. *Transformation*. New York: William Morrow & Co., 1988.

"Sumerian Gods and Goddesses." http://www.crystalinks.com/sumer gods.html. 2016.

Talbot, Anne. "US government implicated in planned theft of Iraqi artistic treasures." http://www.wsws.org/en/articles/2003/04/loot -a19.html. April 19, 2005.

"Taoist Deities/Gods." http://www.taoistsecret.com/taoistgod.html. 2006.

Tellinger, Michael. *African Temples of the Anunnaki*. Rochester, VT: Bear & Company, 2013.

————. *Slave Species of the Gods*. Rochester, VT: Bear & Company, 2012.

Tingley, Katherine. *The Theosophical Path: Illustrated Monthly, Volume 7*. Point Loma, CA: New Century Corporation, 1914.

Tompkins, William Mills. *Selected by Extraterrestrials*. CreateSpace, 2015.

Tonnies, Mac. "Posthuman Blues." http://posthumanblues.blogspot. com/2006/04/of-course-cryptoterrestrials-dont.html. April 16, 2006.

————. *The Cryptoterrestrials*. San Antonio, TX: Anomalist Books, 2010.

Urken, Ross Kenneth. "Doctor Ready To Perform First Human Head Transplant." http://www.newsweek.com/2016/05/06/first-human -head-transplant-452240.html. April 26, 2016.

Vallee, Jacques. *Messengers of Deception*. Brisbane, Australia: Daily Grail Publishing, 2008.

————. *Passport to Magonia*. Chicago, IL: Contemporary Books, 1993.

Von Daniken, Erich. *Odyssey of the Gods*. Element Books, Ltd., 2000.

Wagner, Stephen. "Saint-German: The Immortal Count." http://paranormal.about.com/od/humanenigmas/a/saint-germain.htm. October 23, 2015.

Walton, Travis. *Fire in the Sky*. New York: Marlowe & Co., 1997.

Ward, Dan Sewell. "Are the Extraterrestrials Who First Came to Earth Still Here?" http://www.halexandria.org/dward359.htm. 2003.

———. "White Powder of Gold." http://www.halexandria.org/dward469.htm. 2003.

Wentz-Evans, W.Y. *The Fairy Faith in Celtic Countries*. Pompton Plains, NJ: New Page Books, 2004.

"Were the Anunnaki alien race, the same Hindu gods???" http://www.abovetopsecret.com/forum/thread556312/pg1. March 29, 2010.

West, Michael D. "How Engineered Stem Cells May Enable Youthful Immortality." http://www.lifeextension.com/magazine/2013/2/otc/page-01. February 2013.

"White Powder of Gold (ORME)." http://www.tokenrock.com/explain-white-powder-of-gold--orme--84.html. 2010.

"Who is Manannan Mac Lir?" http://manannan.net/whois/index.html. 2015.

Wilde, F.S. *Ancient Legends of Ireland*. New York: Sterling, 1992.

Woollaston, Victoria. "We'll be uploading our entire MINDS to computers by 2045 and our bodies will be replaced by machines within 90 years, Google expert claims." http://www.dailymail.co.uk/sciencetech/article-2344398/Google-futurist-claims-uploading-entire-MINDS-computers-2045-bodies-replaced-machines-90-years.html. June 19, 2013.

World Revolution. "Bush Cultural Advisers Quit Over Iraq Museum Theft." http://www.worldrevolution.org/article/813. April 17, 2003.

Zeidman, Jennie. *A Helicopter-UFO Encounter over Ohio*. Chicago, IL: Center for UFO Studies, 1979.

INDEX

ABOUT THE AUTHOR

Nick Redfern is the author of more than 30 books on UFOs, Bigfoot, lake monsters, the Abominable Snowman, and Hollywood scandals, including *Weapons of the Gods*; *Bloodline of the Gods*; *Monster Files*; *Memoirs of a Monster Hunter*; *The Real Men in Black*; *The NASA Conspiracies*; *Keep Out!*; *The Pyramids and the Pentagon*; *Contactees*; *The World's Weirdest Places*; *For Nobody's Eyes Only*; and *Close Encounters of the Fatal Kind*. He has appeared on many TV shows, including: Fox News; the BBC's *Out of This World*; the SyFy Channel's *Proof Positive*; the Space Channel's *Fields of Fear*; the History Channel's *Monster Quest*, *America's Book of Secrets*, *Ancient Aliens*, and *UFO Hunters*; Science's *The Unexplained Files*; the National Geographic Channel's *Paranatural*; and MSNBC's *Countdown* with Keith Olbermann. Originally from the UK, Nick lives on the fringes of Dallas, Texas. He can be contacted at his blog: *http://nickredfernfortean.blogspot.com*.